"As a teen, I longed for an assuring voice that said, 'Don't listen to the naysayers, the judgers, the bullies, or the critic in your head—listen to my voice, and I'll point you in the right direction.' In *Liked: Whose Approval Are You Living For?* Kari Kampakis *is* that voice, speaking specifically to teen girls living in the age of screens, external validation, and superficial measures of success. Using relatable anecdotes, thoughtful reflection questions, and biblical references, Kari empowers young women to make sound decisions that will bring them closer to God and His purpose for their lives. *Liked* is truly a first of its kind for teen girls, turning down the artificial noise of their world to emphasize God's true voice of unconditional love and grace."

—Rachel Macy Stafford, *New York Times* bestselling author of *Hands Free Mama* and *Hands Free Life*

"As the mother of a daughter, I am so grateful for Kari Kampakis. Trying to raise kids is like a constantly moving target in today's world, and her wisdom and insight helps and encourages me as I find my way in the parenting journey. *Liked* is a must-read for teenage girls to help them know to find their worth in the things that matter most."

—Melanie Shankle, *New York Times* bestselling author of *Nobody's Cuter Than You*

"What I love about *Liked* is that Kari doesn't just offer advice to teenage girls about how to navigate the insta-culture that they inhabit. Instead, Kari digs into big questions about identity and purpose—*Who am I? What am I here for?*—and as she answers those questions, she continually points her readers to a much deeper truth: they are dearly loved, intentionally made, and wholly accepted by their Creator. Kari's empathy, wisdom, and compassion are gifts to all women, no matter our age, and I'm grateful that, in *Liked*, her life-giving, uplifting, and encouraging words continually remind teenage girls (and the rest of us!) of the joys of relational substance in a culture that can tempt us to settle for superficiality. Mamas, if you're looking for a book to read with your teenage daughter(s), this is it!"

—Sophie Hudson, author of *Giddy Up, Eunice*
and *Home Is Where My People Are*

"As a mom of four growing daughters, I am grateful for the heart, ministry, and words of Kari. In *Liked*, Kari provides tween and teen girls with a combination of honesty and vulnerability that speaks directly into their realities. This is the type of resource I will gladly share with my girls as they navigate the twists and turns of life while keeping their focus on God's eternal truth."

—Wynter Pitts, author of *You're God's Girl!: A Devotional for Tweens*

"Kari Kampakis has written a must-read book for every young woman who longs to be liked. Kari tackles tough questions and real struggles with biblical truth and priceless wisdom, empowering young women to live free from the pressure to pretend they are someone they aren't because they are already loved just as they are! If you want the young women in your life to see themselves through God's lens of grace, give them this book."

—Jeannie Cunnion, author of *Parenting the Wholehearted Child*

"*Liked* is an absolute must-read for teenage girls. In a culture where social media saturates our lives, Kari equips girls with truth regarding identity, acceptance, and authentic relationship. The discussion questions at the end of each chapter make *Liked* the perfect book for a girls' small group or book club."

—Allison Hendrix, writer/blogger at *The House of Hendrix*

"As a counselor for girls and their families for over twenty years, I am grateful for any voice that speaks truth into the lives of girls. It's harder than ever to grow up. And I trust Kari Kampakis's voice to help girls do just that: to grow up anchored to the truth of who God is and how He has designed them to be more than just liked. Thank you, Kari, for directly, graciously, and relevantly voicing the truths that girls today need desperately to hear."

—Sissy Goff, M.Ed., LPC-MHSP, author, speaker, and Director of
Counseling at Daystar Counseling Ministries in Nashville, Tennessee

"*Liked* is a godsend for our youth. We have unwittingly created a culture in which our deepest need to connect, to be understood, and to be accepted can be satisfied instantaneously by our smartphones. Kari Kampakis reminds our youth that the power of social media can and should be used for good, but that true identity is not built online. When we find unearned and lavish approval in God's grace, then—and only then—can we discover our own unique identities."

—Catherine Montgomery, Director of Children's Ministry,
Christ Episcopal Church, Ponte Vedra Beach, Florida

Liked

Whose approval are you living for?

kari kampakis

THOMAS NELSON

Since 1798

Liked

Published in Nashville, Tennessee, by Tommy Nelson. Tommy Nelson is an imprint of Thomas Nelson. Thomas Nelson is a registered trademark of HarperCollins Christian Publishing, Inc.

Published in association with the literary agency of Wolgemuth & Associates, Inc.

Tommy Nelson titles may be purchased in bulk for educational, business, fund-raising, or sales promotional use. For information, please e-mail SpecialMarkets@ThomasNelson.com.

Unless otherwise noted, Scripture quotations are taken from the Holy Bible, New International Version®, NIV®. Copyright © 1973, 1978, 1984, 2011 by Biblica, Inc.® Used by permission of Zondervan. All rights reserved worldwide. www.zondervan.com. The "NIV" and "New International Version" are trademarks registered in the United States Patent and Trademark Office by Biblica, Inc.®

Scripture quotations marked (NLT) are taken from the *Holy Bible*, New Living Translation. © 1996, 2004, 2007, 2013 by Tyndale House Foundation. Used by permission of Tyndale House Publishers, Inc., Carol Stream, Illinois 60188. All rights reserved.

Scripture quotations marked (ESV) are taken from the ESV® Bible (The Holy Bible, English Standard Version®). Copyright © 2001 by Crossway, a publishing ministry of Good News Publishers. Used by permission. All rights reserved.

Scripture quotations marked (NASB) are taken from New American Standard Bible®. Copyright © 1960, 1962, 1963, 1968, 1971, 1972, 1973, 1975, 1977, 1995 by The Lockman Foundation. Used by permission. (www.Lockman.org)

Scripture quotations marked (GNT) are taken from the Good News Translation in Today's English Version—Second Edition. Copyright 1992 by American Bible Society. Used by permission.

ISBN-13: 978-0-7180-8723-4

Library of Congress Cataloging-in-Publication Data

Names: Kampakis, Kari, 1972- author.
Title: Liked : whose approval are you living for? / Kari Kampakis.
Description: Nashville : Thomas Nelson, 2016. | Includes bibliographical references.
Identifiers: LCCN 2016021918 | ISBN 9780718087234 (softcover)
Subjects: LCSH: Teenage girls--Religious life. | Christian teenagers--Religious life. | Self-acceptance--Religious aspects--Christianity. | Teenage girls--Conduct of life.
Classification: LCC BV4551.3 .K364 2016 | DDC 248.8/33--dc23 LC record available at https://lccn.loc.gov/2016021918

Printed in United States

17 18 19 20 RRD 6 5 4 3 2

Mfr: RRD / Crawfordsville, Indiana / November 2016 / PO # 9413164

To my daughters: Camille, Ella, Marie Claire, and Sophie.
May you and the girls of your generation always see
yourselves and others through God's eyes and know how
unconditionally loved you are every second of every day.

Contents

Liked: Whose Approval Are You Living For?

Identity: The real you is better than the false you. Be true to yourself.

Confidence: What people say about you is opinion. What God says about you is fact. The way to know your worth is to focus on the facts.

Kindness: All around you, people are feeling lonely, invisible, and insignificant. Be the girl who takes a genuine interest in others. Spread kindness, love, and compassion.

Character: Through technology, you speak to an audience. Use your voice for good. Be an encourager, not a critic.

Commitment: There's a difference between online friends and real friends. Online friends take two seconds to "like" your latest post. Real friends take off an afternoon to visit you when you need them most.

Connection: Relationships grow deeper through face-to-face interaction. Focus on depth and connections, not numbers and screens.

Wisdom: Being left out or excluded can make you feel rejected and forgotten. Learning to deal wisely with your emotions protects your relationships and self-worth.

Humility: God is calling you to a life of service and active faith, not fame and self-promotion.

Courage: You were made to change the world. Don't let the world change you.

Direction: At the end of the day, only two questions matter: *Am I pleasing God?* and *Do I like who I'm becoming?*

Introduction

Of course you want to be liked—I want to be liked too! And, honestly, there is nothing wrong with that desire. God wired you to live in community with others. He created you to need friends. He wants you to cultivate strong relationships that bring you joy and draw you closer to Him.

But the problem with wanting to be liked is that it can take your eyes off God. It can lead you to make choices based on what's *popular* rather than what's *right*. And when your desire to please people overpowers your desire to please God, issues arise. You may experience a slow drift away from God that is so subtle you barely even notice it.

So take a moment to ask yourself two questions: *Whose approval am I living for?* and *Do I care more about what my friends and other people think of me or what God knows about me?*

········•··•····•··•··•···•···•····•··•·· ♥ ·······••·····•·······••·····•·····••·····

Am I now trying to win the approval of
human beings, or of God? Or am I trying to
please people? If I were still trying to please
people, I would not be a servant of Christ.

—GALATIANS 1:10

··•····•·····•··•···•··••···•·•···•··••···•···•·····•····•··•·····••····

xiii

No matter how you answer, this book is for you. So find a cozy place to kick back, and let's discover together what it means to live confidently in God's love, truth, and grace.

The Lure of Applause

In our world of show-offs, one common mindset is to go big or go home.

We girls discover early on that embellishing one's appearance, personality, and public persona can attract instant attention and applause. The more we're "on," the more people tend to like us.

So we learn to put on a show. We learn to smile, shine, and keep up a perfect act. The way people cheer us on, we figure we're doing something right. We assume we're on the right track.

But constantly playing to a crowd has a cost that *will* catch up with us. It manifests as exhaustion, stress, burnout, anxiety, and desperation. To constantly perform and always be "on" is hard work. It can chip away at our confidence and make us want to withdraw.

The good news, my friend, is you have a choice. *You don't have to waste your time and energy trying to constantly bedazzle an audience.* The only audience who really matters is your audience of One. And, believe it or not, He adores *the real you.* No masks, no filters, no tricks.

God loves you exactly as you are today. And when He looks at you, He sees beauty and potential.

Regardless of whether the world considers you special or treats you as simply another face in the crowd, God believes in you. He is your biggest fan, and more than anything else, He wants you to rest in Him.

·····•·•···•·•···•···•···•···•······ ♥ ·····•·•···•··•····•·····•······•·•··

Constantly playing to a crowd has a cost that
will catch up with us. It manifests as exhaustion,
stress, burnout, anxiety, and desperation.

··•·•····•·•···•··•···•···•···•····•·····•·····•··•·····•···•··•···•·····•·•··

Would You Rather Be Liked and Noticed—or Loved and Known?

While traveling around to talk about my first book, *10 Ultimate Truths Girls Should Know*, I quickly noticed the topic that teen and tween girls today seem to struggle with most.

In every city I visited and every group I spoke with, most girls' questions boiled down to one subject. It wasn't boys, self-esteem, or fashion they wanted to discuss. No, what these girls had on their minds was something I never knew was such an issue.

And that is: *friendship*. How to find good friends, how to handle a mean culture, and what to do when friends hurt, reject, or betray you.

Many questions broke my heart. They also opened my eyes to the needs of today's girls. So when I started writing this book, I knew exactly what I wanted to cover in detail.

One of my primary goals in the pages ahead is to illustrate the art of friendship. Using both fictional stories and real-life examples, I hope to get you thinking about your relationships and the direction in which they're headed.

Is it fun to be liked and noticed? Absolutely. But what your heart really craves, the desire that runs deeply and quietly below the surface, is to be loved and known.

And since feeling loved and known begins with understanding

your identity in Jesus Christ—God's only Son, "the way and the truth and the life" (John 14:6)—He is the reference point for this book.

Growing closer to God is really a matter of becoming more like Christ. As you learn to love the way Jesus loves and put into practice the character traits He models, God's will for you becomes more evident. Becoming more like Christ enables you to find peace, joy, and security even in difficult times.

Making God your top priority also helps you attract the right people into your life and experience the right kind of applause. Then, more than feeling liked, you can feel loved. Of course, for relationships to work, you must work on your relationships. This means loving your people well, both in person and online.

So let's thank God for this opportunity to come together, and let's praise Him in advance for the plans He has for you, particularly those meaningful connections that will reveal His amazing grace and give you the sense of belonging your heart longs for.

Your sister in Christ,

Kari

1

Identity

>>> The real you is better than the
       false you. Be true to yourself. <<<

Every morning when Alexis woke up, she felt the same familiar pressure.

Pressure to dress up.

Pressure to look stunning.

Pressure to be perfect, flawless, and amazing.

There was a time when Alexis enjoyed getting ready for school. She loved trying the newest makeup tutorial, styling her hair, and putting together new outfits.

But now? Now it all felt like a chore. As soon as Alexis opened her eyes, a familiar dread set in. She was tired of all the effort required to live up to her image. She was tired of the lifestyle she'd inadvertently created for herself.

Her gripe sounded so shallow and vain, and that's why Alexis didn't discuss this with anyone. Who wanted to hear the supposed "It" girl complain about the time and energy it took to meet everyone's expectations? Even her mom couldn't help because she would just tell Alexis to drop her morning routine if it no longer made her happy.

1

But Alexis was scared to drop it because then people might drop *her*. And despite what her grades in chemistry suggested, Alexis wasn't dumb. She knew why boys paid attention to her. She understood why girls sought her advice, copied her style, and wanted to be her friend.

In matters of beauty and fashion, Alexis was the expert. And though she wasn't sure how she'd earned this reputation or when she'd become the school trendsetter, she did like being known for something. It felt good to have people respect her opinion, listen to her, and anxiously await her arrival at events to see what look she'd pulled off this time.

Being the "It" girl had been fun, but Alexis was over it. All the compliments and praise were starting to sound empty and trite. Deep down, she longed for more. She knew change was in order, but she questioned whether she could handle the consequences.

After all, right now she was a *Somebody*. And altering the lifestyle that seemed to work for everyone but her might make her a *Nobody*.

Alexis also wondered if turning over a new leaf was even possible. Would anyone take her seriously if she talked less about the hot new nail polish and more about dreams, hopes, and goals? What if her friends wanted the old Alexis back? What if they found the new Alexis dull and boring?

In some weird, unexplainable way, Alexis felt like a prisoner in her own body. She was trapped in a routine out of habit and fear,

••••••••••••••••••••••••••••• ♥ •••••••••••••••••••••••••••••

God is working in you, giving you the desire and the power to do what pleases him.

—PHILIPPIANS 2:13 NLT

••

helpless until the day she would become brave enough to finally break the cycle.

Her dream was to wake up one morning with her mind and body at ease. She wanted relief from these bells and whistles that others expected from her and the courage to be her most honest, natural self.

The Truth About Identity

If you think about it, you can become almost anyone you want to be. You can take on any identity imaginable. The possibilities are endless.

It's freeing to have so many choices, isn't it? Yet at the same time, the number of choices can be overwhelming. Sometimes you need help narrowing down the options. You need a starting point and some clues to point you in the right direction and create a vision for your life.

Typically, your search for identity begins in your immediate environment. You watch your parents and think about, and perhaps copy, what you see. You look at the people around you and make mental notes about what they value, the choices they make, who they form relationships with, and how happy—or terrible—their lives seem.

You may also look at popular culture and your current favorite celebrities. Whoever you're drawn to, whoever inspires you, whoever you relate to most—these tend to become the role models who you notice, study, and emulate.

Throughout your identity-searching process, you'll ask yourself questions. Your questions may sound like these as you try to decode your inner mystery:

♡ *Who do I want to be like?*
♡ *Who do I not want to be like?*
♡ *Whose life looks appealing?*
♡ *Whose life does not look appealing?*
♡ *Who shares my passions?*
♡ *Whose footsteps would I like to follow?*
♡ *Who do I have a lot in common with?*
♡ *Who can I see myself becoming?*

At some point in this process, another dynamic comes into play. You begin picking up on how other people perceive you and receive you. You draw conclusions about what they think of you by the way they talk to you, treat you, and see you.

This external feedback plays a *huge* role in shaping your self-image. For better or for worse, you're likely to internalize what you hear as well as the messages people convey through verbal and nonverbal clues.

♡ *That girl said I'm beautiful. I must be a beautiful person.*
♡ *That girl looked at me with disgust. I must be a disgusting person.*
♡ *That boy said he loved me. I must be a lovable person.*
♡ *That boy treated me as if I'm worthless. I must be a worthless person.*

In some situations, noticing how people respond to you is useful. It can help you hone your social skills and allow you to recognize areas where you may have room to improve.

At the same time, it's easy to overanalyze everyone's reaction to you—and sometimes come to the wrong conclusion about yourself. It's tempting to let the approval or disapproval of others shape the way you think about yourself and determine the identity you choose.

Whatever version of you people seem to like best—well, that's who you strive to become. Or you may test-drive different identities until you find one that strikes a chord and gets you noticed, praised, and accepted.

Letting people determine who you should be, however, turns you into a people-pleaser. It leads you to rely on human affirmation instead of God's. As His quiet voice gets drowned out by public opinion, you may lose touch with what you know deep down is most important. You may not see a problem because, with all the cheering you hear from people around you, everything seems fine.

But you can be on the wrong track and still get cheered on wildly. You can make a big mistake and still have some people smiling and patting you on the back.

For this reason, among others, you can't depend solely on external clues to shape your identity. After all, people sometimes get it wrong. People sometimes tell lies that ultimately hurt you. People may encourage you to make choices and build an identity that reflects the values of the world, not the will of God.

Slowly but surely, these choices can separate you from God. They create a gap between who you are and who you're called to be as a child of the Lord.

······················· ♥ ·······························

Letting people determine who you should be, however, turns you into a people-pleaser. It leads you to rely on human affirmation instead of God's.

···

Let Jesus Be Your Rock

So what's a girl to do? How do you begin learning who you truly are?

According to God, your starting point and focal point should be Jesus. Since Jesus is unchanging, since He is "the same yesterday and today and forever" (Hebrews 13:8), He's the rock that you can build your life on.

Overnight you can lose everything the world tells you to base your identity on: your talents, your appearance, your friends, your wardrobe, your possessions, even your Instagram account. You can be stripped of all the earthly trappings that we humans tend to put our faith in.

But what *nobody* can take away is your status as a child of God and the promise of heaven you have through your relationship with Jesus. In Christ, you have the hope of eternal life. You have a joy to cling to in all circumstances.

Even if life pulls the rug out from under you, even if your worst nightmare comes true, you'll still be standing with Jesus when you make Him the foundation of your life.

With Jesus as your rock, the basis of your identity, you can

Do not conform to the pattern of this world, but be transformed by the renewing of your mind. Then you will be able to test and approve what God's will is— his good, pleasing and perfect will.

—ROMANS 12:2

confidently live the life of virtue that God has planted in your heart. You won't have to fear rejection or hustle for human approval because God's unconditional love provides all the approval you need.

As you accept God's love and affirmation, you grow more capable of loving others. You can take the love that God gives you and *pass it on*. Doing this makes you the kind of person people want to be around because love is magnetic.

Real freedom begins with knowing the truth. By basing your identity search on the truth and letting the Holy Spirit—God's presence in you—guide you, the real you can emerge. You will find the freedom to be who God created you to be.

It's Hard to Love Someone You Don't Know

So much is said these days about the importance of being "real," "vulnerable," and "transparent."

Even so, these qualities can be difficult to find—especially online where it's easy to project a glossy identity. Facebook is often called "Fakebook" because people tend to share only their best moments, and we buy into the illusion that other people's lives are consistently perfect.

We know this is impossible, of course, but the pictures tell a different story.

The truth is, we love it when other people are real. We appreciate the courage and honesty that being genuine requires, and we wish more people would do the same.

But when it comes to pulling back the curtain on our own lives, we hesitate. We're scared to admit our flaws or show our weaknesses. We're convinced that if people knew the real scoop about us, they wouldn't like us anymore. They'd be unimpressed or disappointed.

So what do we do instead of being genuine? We put on masks. We perfect our appearance. We dress ourselves up and hide anything that may reveal or be perceived as an imperfection.

Why? Because our world puts shiny, perfect girls on a pedestal. In our media-obsessed culture, being beautiful quickly gets a girl noticed. And the prettier and more perfect a girl appears, the higher her pedestal rises. She attracts more attention, more applause, and more special treatment.

And though we all know that inner beauty is more important than outer beauty, a girl doesn't receive any fanfare when her heart grows more beautiful. Boys don't whistle as she passes by. Girls don't tell her that she looks *fabulous*. People don't obsess over her pictures on social media and gush about how GOR-GEOUS her heart is.

Here's the kicker: during this stage of life, when you're fast approaching your physical peak, the applause for physical perfection rings loudest. You face intense pressure to invest more in your outward appearance than your inner life, prioritizing show over substance.

Sadly, what many people are most eager to know about you are answers to questions like these:

♡ Who are your friends?
♡ Who is your boyfriend?
♡ What kind of car do you (or will you) drive?
♡ What brands of clothing do you wear?
♡ What part of town do you live in?
♡ How many followers do you have on social media?
♡ What's the highest number of "likes" you've ever gotten?

Is it shallow and superficial for people to care so much about your exterior package? Yes.

Is it unfortunate that we live in an age of sound bites and thin-slicing, when you have seven seconds or less to make a good impression and when people make snap judgments about you with little information? Of course it is.

Is it unfair that people take a quick mental snapshot of who they *think* you are and define you by what's evident on the outside, depriving you of the chance to reveal yourself at a deeper level? Definitely.

But your best defense, I believe, is awareness. Be aware of what you're dealing with. Accept now that you'll encounter many people who care more about those fabulous shoes you're wearing or the pretty house you live in than what is stirring in your heart.

They'd rather talk about the size of your figure or the cost of your homecoming dress than your hopes, fears, and disappointments.

Bracing yourself for our culture's preoccupation with presentation can help you avoid buying into its superficiality. It helps you understand in advance the dangers of defining yourself by the world's values and cultivating a false you—the girl who may look super impressive . . . yet at the expense of a neglected soul.

••••••••••••••••••••••••••••••• ♥ •••••••••••••••••••••••••••••••

They traded the truth about God for a lie.
So they worshiped and served the things
God created instead of the Creator himself,
who is worthy of eternal praise! Amen.
—ROMANS 1:25 NLT

••

Do You Want a Life of Meaning— or a Life of Attention?

Remember Alexis in the opening story? Like many girls, Alexis mistakenly believed her looks were her best asset. She'd built an identity for herself based on eyelash curlers, spray tans, and fashion statements.

But even if you're a showstopper like Alexis, you have so much more to offer the world than advice about how to look amazing. To believe otherwise is to sell yourself short.

Like Alexis, you must overcome any fear of people not liking you if you drop the act. *You must remember that real relationships begin with your being real because people can't love someone they don't know.*

Just because your friends know how talented a gymnast you are or how much you love Lilly Pulitzer doesn't mean they really *know* you. Simply knowing these facts about you isn't enough for them to build a rich and dynamic relationship with you.

To be deeply loved and known, you have to dig deeper. This means thinking about what's below the surface and sharing your heart with people who have earned your trust and respect.

The real you wants a life of meaning. The false you settles for a life of attention.

The real you doesn't need materialism. The false you is consumed by it.

The real you worships God. The false you worships yourself.

The real you sees with the heart. The false you trusts only the eye's opinion.

The real you lives with eternity in mind. The false you lives in waiting for the latest and greatest Tory Burch bag.

Decide now which "you" you want to be. Identify in your own life any actions, thoughts, and habits that cultivate the real you versus the false you—and nurture those positives.

Nobody ever figures it out perfectly. Fighting the urge to chase human approval over God's approval is a lifelong battle, and we all occasionally make the mistake of cultivating a false identity at the expense of our real one.

But the good news is, God is gracious. He gives new mercies each morning (Lamentations 3:22–23). God understands your temptations and pressures, and He knows how challenging it is to rise above the world's idea of female perfection.

You are better than the splashy image our world pushes on you and your friends, and with prayer and determination, you can avoid buying into it. You can build your identity on things that matter and discover your self-worth by being uniquely, wonderfully you.

··•····•••··•••··•·••··•·••··•·••·· ♥ ··•••··••··•••••··••··•·••··••••··•· ··

Fearing people is a dangerous trap, but trusting the LORD means safety.
—PROVERBS 29:25 NLT

··•····•••··••·····•·•••··•·•••··•••••··•••··••··•·•••··••·····•·•••··•••••··•• ··

Staying True to Yourself

My friend Sophie Hudson works with teenage girls in Birmingham, Alabama. A beloved author, blogger, and speaker, Sophie has a huge heart for girls and amazing insight into their thought lives.

At the high school where she works, Sophie helped start a program called SOS: Stack Our Stones & Share Our Stories. She invites girls who have graduated to share their testimonies with the younger girls.

Their testimonies usually reflect this theme: "Here's what my life looked like on the outside . . . and here's what was really happening on the inside."

What Sophie recognizes is the healing power of sharing our insecurities and misguided quests. Besides building character, being vulnerable builds community and helps others. It breaks down walls and gives other girls permission to be honest. What results is an environment where girls can relax and be real.

And isn't that what we all dream of? Don't we all crave a safe place where we can be ourselves and share whatever is on our hearts?

Please note the key words here are *safe place*. Particularly when it comes to sharing your innermost thoughts, I advise you to use discretion regarding who you share them with and where you do it.

As you can imagine, some people would love to twist your words around and use them against you. They'd like to prey on what you share as your vulnerabilities and weak points.

For this reason, among others, I strongly suggest that you don't post your deepest, darkest secrets on social media in the name of being "real." I wouldn't air your dirty laundry or publicly share the most private details of your life.

The fact is, some details and life moments should remain private. They should be reserved for a close circle of people you fully trust—like your mom, dad, sister, brother, best friend, cousin, counselor, or someone else who loves you and respects you enough to keep your private matters private.

Eventually you may be ready to share the story of your adolescent years. But right now, your story is unfolding. It's still taking shape as you discover who you are both individually and as part of a bigger community.

The good news is, now is the perfect time to cultivate the real you. Now is the time to peel back the layers and explore who you are below the surface. With your identity search just starting, you're not too set in your ways, and you haven't mastered the art of pretending to be someone you're not.

So take advantage of this opportunity to be honest with yourself and think about the identity you hope to grow into.

••••••••••••••••••••••••••••••• ❤ •••••••••••••••••••••••••••••••

Some details and life moments should remain private. They should be reserved for a close circle of people you fully trust.

••

≫≫― ••• ♡ ••• ―≪≪

Five Ways to Cultivate the Real You

Cultivating the real you requires you to trust God and listen to His voice.

God designed you to live for Him, and the identity that feels best—the one that will bring you the greatest peace and joy—will always be one that reflects His values and character.

With that said, here are five ideas to help you develop the real you.

1. Focus on what money can't buy. Money itself isn't bad, but the love of money is. In fact, 1 Timothy 6:10 names the love of money as "a root of all kinds of evil."

Why is the love of money so destructive? Because it takes your eyes off God. It distracts you from your faith. It can focus your attention on material goals that feed your ego—*Shopping sprees! Luxury vacations! A rich boyfriend whose family is loaded!*—rather than spiritual goals that feed your soul.

While people look at appearances, God looks at your heart (1 Samuel 16:7). He cares more about how well you treat people than how much you impress them.

Adopting God's priorities helps you tap into the real you. You'll learn to see the difference between things that can bring temporary happiness—like getting a pedicure—and things that can bring lasting joy—like making a new friend or teaching a child to read.

2. Look for light. Have you ever thought about what makes a flower bloom? After it's watered, what prompts a flower to open up and reveal its authentic beauty?

The answer is *light*. As a flower responds to light, it stretches up toward the sun and serves its God-given purpose by growing into its full potential.

People are the same way. We need light in order to bloom. And in a dark world like ours, light can be difficult to find. This is why God gave us His Son: because Jesus *is* light. He's "the light of the world" who saves us from walking in darkness (John 8:12).

The amount of light you expose yourself to is really a matter of how much Jesus you expose yourself to. Do you pray and read your Bible? Do you go to church and let the message of the gospel influence your thoughts, habits, and actions? Do you spend time with people who live by faith and learn from them?

If so, you're on the right track. If not, seek more light in your life. All of us need more light than we have. All of us need more Jesus to cultivate our real self.

3. Leave free time in your schedule. As a society, we're too busy. We've made busyness both an epidemic and a status symbol. Even at your age, you face intense pressure to pack your calendar so you can stay competitive and avoid idleness.

Parents often say, "Keeping my child busy keeps them out of trouble." Though there is some truth to that statement, I agree with the many psychologists and counselors who claim this generation of teenagers is the most stressed out and depressed they've ever seen, largely because they're overbooked, overwhelmed, and exhausted by our culture's unrealistic expectations.[1]

Please understand that I'm not advocating laziness. Both you and I are called to be responsible citizens, and in every stage of life God wants us to give our best (Colossians 3:23–24).

At the same time, your body and mind require downtime. You need opportunities to rest, relax, and reflect.

Even Jesus frequently went away by Himself to pray and spend time with God. Downtime is helpful to your identity search because it allows you to let your guard down, drop any pretense, and discover the real you. It offers space for you to enjoy activities for the simple pleasure of doing them rather than to achieve a specific goal.

So consider how you feel when you play ball with your dog, walk on the beach at sunset, or bake a pie from scratch with your grandmother. Think about how your heart feels when you and your friends have a water balloon fight or when you doodle in your journal and daydream about the children's books you hope to illustrate someday.

The clues you pick up about yourself during a rest period are very telling. When you're relaxed and comfortable, the real you feels safe to come out without fear of judgment or rejection.

4. Invest in friends who like the real you. One reason why girls cultivate false identities is to impress the wrong people.

Remember when I said that some girls care more about the shoes on your feet than the feelings in your heart? Well, if they become your closest friends, their values and attitudes will influence you. You'll be very tempted to join them in chasing superficial goals.

Though it's good to be kind to these girls—*be kind to everyone*— don't overinvest in these relationships. Keep your expectations in check and know that you may not have many meaningful conversations.

Friendships with superficial people tend to be, well, superficial and unsatisfying. More than that, these friendships hold you back. You'll never find the courage to be yourself if you're surrounded by people who can't appreciate the real you and who you are at your core.

Being superficial attracts superficial friends. Being real attracts real friends. So be intentional about building friendships that feed your soul, draw you to God, and bring out your best side.

5. Choose an accountability partner. As you get older, you're more likely to hold back your innermost thoughts and feelings. You'll learn to smile when your heart is breaking and look together when you're falling apart.

Sometimes circumstances will require you to put on a brave face, act strong, or save your breakdown until you're behind closed doors. Even so, I hope you never lose the ability and courage to admit—*in the right company*—what's really going on inside you.

Having an accountability partner helps keep you honest. It gives you a sounding board and a steel vault for what you openly share from your heart.

Whatever mistakes you make, you admit them. Whatever trials or temptations you face, you discuss them. Whatever struggles you overcome, you celebrate them. Your accountability partner does the same with you.

When choosing an accountability partner, look for a girl who is wise, godly, and trustworthy. Be sure she cares about her relationship with God and looks to Him for her sense of value. Commit to speaking the truth to each other in love and to making spiritual growth—as well as healthy identity formation—your end goals.

· · ·•· · · · · · ·•· · · · · ·•· · · · · ·•· · · · ·•· · · · · ❤ · · · · · · · ·•· · · · · ·•· · · · · · · · · ·•· · · · ·•· · · ·

"My sheep listen to my voice; I know them, and they follow me."

—JOHN 10:27 NLT

· · ·•· · · · · · ·•· · · · · ·•· · · · · ·•· · · · ·•· · · ·•· · · · ·•· · · · · · · · ·•· · · · · · · · ·•· · · · · · · ·•· · · · ·•· · · ·

Are You Building Your Identity on a Rock—or Quicksand?

The topic of identity can be summed up with a few key points.

You are special because you exist—*period.*

You have inherent worth and dignity because you are God's child—*period.*

Nothing you do or accomplish can make God value you more. *He already loves you at maximum capacity.* Whether or not you accept His love and let it impact your life is your personal choice.

You can choose any identity you want. You can experiment with every identity under the sun. Not all identities will bring you peace, however. Not all identities will make you feel good about yourself or launch your life in a meaningful direction.

Our world will encourage you to build your identity on quicksand. It will tell you to base your self-worth on your body, your relationships, your accomplishments, or your latest performance.

But please remember, these earthly trappings can change or disappear overnight. If you believe your dance skills make you special and suddenly you can't dance anymore because you break your leg, does that mean you're worthless? What will happen, then, if your whole life revolves around dance?

God's most important commandment is to keep Him first (Exodus 20:2–3). One reason He wants to be the center of your universe is because it helps you avoid taking a *good* thing in your life—like dance—and making it the *best* thing.

Putting God first allows you to enjoy your God-given gifts without basing your confidence on them. Putting God first eases your fear of losing your gifts because even if that happened, you'd still have the most ultimate blessing.

Jesus.

Jesus is the rock you can count on as you wrestle with your identity. If you're worried about rejection and people not liking the real you, remember that Jesus knows you completely and isn't turned off by a single weakness. Even your worst flaw can't push Him away.

The One who knows you best also loves you best. He is passionate about *you.* So trust God to tell you exactly who you are. Take your identity search to Him, and let Him fill you with the courage to be the girl He created you to be.

················· ♥ ·················

You have inherent worth and dignity because you are God's child—*period.*

··

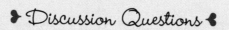

❧ *Discussion Questions* ☙

1. What are you basing your identity on? What role models have shaped your sense of self?

2. Name three people who like the real you. Does their acceptance encourage you to be real with others? Why or why not?

3. Social media makes it easy to build a false identity online. What are some consequences of this?

4. Think of a social situation in which you pretended to be someone you're not. What led you to do that? How did you feel afterward?

5. When, if ever, have you been burned by showing your real self? What did you learn from that experience?

6. What can you do to encourage other girls to be real? How can you build a community where everyone feels safe being real?

2

Confidence

 What people say about you is
opinion. What God says about
you is fact. The way to know your
worth is to focus on the facts.

It was a great weekend for Emma—the best one she'd had in years.

On Saturday morning Emma's family went to eat breakfast at the Pancake House. It turned out to be a surprise birthday party for Emma. Her ten best friends were waiting for her with hats, confetti, horns, and balloons.

For two hours, they filled the restaurant with squeals and laughter. And when everyone sang "Happy Birthday," Emma felt unbelievably loved.

And then on Saturday night, Emma and her band played at a community crawfish boil that drew two thousand people. They played on the main stage and opened up for a big local act.

Emma had never sung in front of a crowd that size, and when she noticed a group of boys and girls from school among the sea of faces, her stomach knotted up. She regretted saying yes to singing at this event.

Once the music started, however, Emma's nerves faded. She loved singing, performing, and connecting with people through music. Based on their applause, the audience really liked her band. The band members sang, danced, and engaged the crowd, and when the final set was over, people rushed to Emma and told her she did great.

Yes, it was a weekend of exciting highs. And maybe that's what made Monday such a devastating blow.

Of course it was Jill who delivered the blow. A former friend, she knew how to hurt Emma. Even though Emma knew better, she listened to Jill anyway.

"I heard your band the other night," Jill said, leaning against a locker as Emma pulled her books out. "You're good."

"Thanks," Emma replied, thankful she hadn't seen Jill in the crowd because that would have made her even more nervous.

"You're really brave, you know. Especially when people talk about your lips."

"My lips?" Emma looked at Jill. "What about my lips?"

"It's nothing, really." Jill shrugged her shoulders. "Some guys were just saying that when you sing, you get funny-looking fish lips. They look inflatable like a cartoon character. They made jokes about reeling you in."

"What else did they say?" Emma asked, trying not to cry.

"What does it matter? I told them to quit being mean. They're idiots anyway. Don't listen to those jerks."

Emma had more questions, but she couldn't give Jill the satisfaction of thinking she cared. Jill knew that Emma had always thought that, compared to the rest of her face, her lips were huge. Emma could handle hating her own lips, but hearing that others had noticed them made her want to crawl under a rock and hide her face forever.

Emma could have kicked herself for giving Jill's words the power to hurt her. Now her mind was spinning. She was officially freaking out.

Should she quit singing? Was this band a terrible idea? Were people still talking about her lips? Even though Emma loved music, the thought of getting on stage again made her panic. Why put herself in a position where people could pick her apart? Why open herself up to criticism?

Just this morning Emma had been so happy. Savoring the events of the weekend, she'd practically floated to school. Now she felt like dirt. She was the punch line to a joke—a joke told to her by someone she couldn't stand, but one that hurt all the same.

········· ♥ ·········

You are altogether beautiful, my
darling; there is no flaw in you.
—SONG OF SONGS 4:7

········· ·········

Know Your Worth

You have undoubtedly discovered by now that people can be mean. If you haven't experienced a dose of meanness yet, unfortunately you probably will.

I wish I could promise that you'll forget every cutting remark. I wish I could assure you that flippant statements like "You only made the basketball team because your dad is friends with the coach" or "You're so skinny, but you're shaped like a pear" will roll off your shoulders and leave you unaffected, but I can't.

Mean comments *will* affect you. They'll stay in your brain, and they'll hurt your heart. Even if you know a statement isn't true, even if you're tough, the words and opinions of others can make you doubt yourself.

But the key word here is *opinions*. What other people say and think about you is their *opinion*. And opinions can be so random. They are wildly unpredictable, ranging from A to Z.

On their own, opinions have no staying power. They can last a long time in our memories, but in real life they're fleeting and constantly changing. That's why basing your confidence and self-worth on people's opinions sets you up for heartache and confusion. It places you at the mercy of other people and whatever mood they're in.

God wants you to base your self-concept on facts. He wants His timeless truths, spelled out in the Bible, to be the words embedded in your heart.

Only God's words have stability and staying power. Only His words have survived for thousands of years and will last through eternity.

Learning Scripture helps you understand yourself and God. It equips you to counter any criticism you hear with His truth and wisdom.

Basing your confidence and self-worth on people's opinions sets you up for heartache and confusion.

God Is Love

Your most dangerous critic—the one who can totally destroy your psyche and sense of reason—is your inner critic.

What you believe about yourself—and what you allow that voice between your ears to tell you—will deeply affect whether you love yourself or whether you hold yourself captive in a mental prison built from lies.

Remember, God is love (1 John 4:8). And when God speaks, He speaks with love. So if the voice in your head is bashing you with put-downs, that isn't God speaking. Insults are never conducive to a healthy thought life, and God would never use tactics like shame, condemnation, or self-loathing to shape the way you see yourself.

What you do with your thoughts—especially negative thoughts—is important. Do you dwell on them, or do you get rid of them? Do you give your inner critic a megaphone, or do you work to silence it? Do you blindly accept people's opinions of you, or do you educate yourself about God's truth so you know what to believe and what to dismiss?

Like Emma in the opening story, you may feel tempted sometimes to internalize discouraging opinions. You may repeat them until you eventually want to give up on yourself or quit your passion. But when you give up or quit, you can't serve God. You hide your talents instead of growing them and using them to point people to Him.

Hearing God's voice is largely a matter of opening your heart and mind to Him. When you're receptive to God, you become familiar with His ways. You learn to recognize the lies and half-truths of the world and redirect negative thoughts into healthy thoughts that bring peace, joy, and freedom.

Only God knows the complete truth about you because He *is* truth and He created you (John 14:6). And while it does take effort to remind yourself of how God sees you, it's well worth it, my friend. *You're worth it.*

In God's eyes you are priceless. Your life has tremendous value and purpose.

·············· ♥ ··············

We are God's handiwork, created in Christ Jesus to do good works, which God prepared in advance for us to do.

—EPHESIANS 2:10

···························

Quick Quiz: Do You Let People Ruin Your Day?

Imagine yourself with a sudden bout of acne. Bumps cover your forehead, and your appointment with the dermatologist is still a week away.

Although you're very self-conscious, your parents make you attend a family dinner. They promise it will lift your spirits, but it doesn't. Because the first person you see as you walk into your grandmother's house is Uncle Jim. He thinks he's funny, but his jokes are always at someone's expense.

"Hey, kid!" he says, smiling and then frowning as you approach. "Whoa! What's up with your face?"

"It's nothing," you reply. "Just a little breakout."

"Little?!" Uncle Jim cackles. "It looks like you've got chicken pox!" Amused by himself, Uncle Jim calls his twin boys into the room. He points to your forehead.

"You see this, boys?" he says. "That's what you get to look forward to!"

"Eww, gross!" your three-year-old cousins reply. They stare at you with a mix of disgust and curiosity. When one twin starts singing, "Creepy, creepy bumps," the other twin dances.

You've held it together until now, but their teasing crushes you. You burst into tears, run down the hall, and lock yourself in your grandmother's bedroom to escape your dysfunctional family.

What do you do next?

A) You get on social media and insult your uncle. You talk about his bad breath, his huge belly, and his inability to hold down a job because he's lazy.

B) You let yourself cry and feel the pain. Your uncle was insensitive and mean, and you decide to never treat anyone the way he treated you. As you think about the people who get teased about problems that can't be fixed with acne medicine, you feel compassion. You realize how this experience may make you kinder to them and others. For that, you're actually grateful.

C) You stay in your grandmother's room all night, refusing to come out even when there is cake and ice cream to celebrate your grandparents' anniversary.

D) You pray and remind yourself that God loves you. Even on your worst days, He thinks you're beautiful. As you repeat this truth from Psalm 139:14—*I am fearfully and wonderfully made*—you think about how inconsequential your acne is compared to God's massive love for you.

If you answered B or D, you're on the right track. You're gaining the perspective to filter criticism in a way that won't ruin your day or your self-esteem.

Though you can't control how people treat you,
you can control whether you take their mean words and
hurtful actions to heart. Having confidence in who you
are because of the One who made you will help you work
through any painful encounter.

Trust the Truth

Everything you need to know about your identity and your value can be found in Scripture. The Bible is God's love letter to you, full of wisdom and life-changing truth.

Since the Bible is a big and sometimes intimidating book, I've compiled a list of truths related to self-worth. Consider this a starting point—a list to add to, reflect upon, and embrace.

♡ *I am made in God's image (Genesis 1:26–28), and I have great potential to become more like Him and reflect His goodness to others.*

♡ *God is within me, so I will not fall (Psalm 46:5).*

♡ *Nothing can separate me from the love of God (Romans 8:39).*

♡ *God has begun a good work in me, and He'll continue that work until the day Jesus returns (Philippians 1:6).*

♡ *God's love toward me is great (Psalm 86:13).*

♡ *The pain I feel now can't compare to the joy that is coming (Romans 8:18).*

♡ *God's plan for me is worth the wait (Jeremiah 29:11).*

♡ *Everything God makes, including me, is good (Genesis 1:31).*

♡ *What people mean for evil against me, God can use for good (Genesis 50:20).*

♡ *I can confidently trust the Lord to take care of me. I don't need to fear bad news (Psalm 112:7).*

♡ *My weaknesses are opportunities to depend on Christ (2 Corinthians 12:9).*

♡ *Jesus looks for me when I'm lost (Matthew 18:12–14).*

♡ *God created me to shine for Him (Matthew 5:14–16).*

While God's words are trustworthy and unchangeable, people are fickle, and their words can be unpredictable. People can love you one day and hate you the next. They can sing your praises or curse your name.

If you rely on people to make you feel good about yourself, you also grant them the power to crush you. You make them the authority in your life.

Let God be that authority instead. Entrust that power to Him. The opinions that seem so important right now are really meaningless in the grand scheme of life.

This doesn't mean that the negative opinions people have don't hurt—they do! But people don't decide where your soul will spend eternity. People can't alter the facts about your worth. And people can't sway God to their way of thinking about you or make Him change His mind about you.

I am convinced that nothing can ever separate us from God's love. Neither death nor life, neither angels nor demons, neither our fears for today nor our worries about tomorrow—not even the powers of hell can separate us from God's love.

—ROMANS 8:38 NLT

God's truths are still true regardless of whether people like them, accept them, or agree with them. You are still His masterpiece whether everyone you know is in consensus or God stands alone.

Isn't that refreshing? Isn't it easier to love yourself when you know His love is guaranteed? When people's words hurt you, let God's words heal you. Take to heart His promises—and remember that He has the final say.

If God Is for You, Who Can Be Against You?

A while back I received a letter from a teenage girl who read my first book and wanted to share the impact it had on her.

One sentence in particular jumped off the page and still resonates with me: "I walk through the halls of my school thinking, *If God is for me, who can be against me?*"

My friend, that is the confidence I want you to have. That is the certainty I hope you'll carry with you everywhere you go.

When you leave home each morning, God doesn't get left behind, locked inside your Bible until you open it again. No, the Lord walks before you and with you (Deuteronomy 31:8). He's as real in public spaces as He is in the privacy of your bedroom.

So welcome God into your everyday life. Be aware of His presence as He empowers you to be a light in this world. If you face a tough critic, remember you're a warrior. Put on the armor of God (Ephesians 6:10–18), and let His truths about your value guard your heart.

Being confident of God's love helps you develop thick skin but keep a tender heart. Confidence in His love enables you to be resilient on the outside yet stay soft inside, capable of responding to people like Christ would no matter how they treat you.

So approach each day determined to stay strong in knowing God loves you. Repeat to yourself a truth that honors God and reminds you of His love, such as:

♡ *Today I'll rely on Jesus to give me strength.*
♡ *I'm confident that God loves me and lives in me.*
♡ *My Lord is my protector.*

As a child of God, you have every reason to walk with your head held high. You have nothing to fear or prove. Since God is for you, no one can diminish your worth. Since God lives in you, no one can take away your hope of eternal life.

Opinions may come and go, but God's words—about your value and His love for you—last forever. So set your mind on His facts, keep His truths close to your heart, and repeat them to yourself as often as necessary.

Being confident of God's love helps you develop thick skin but keep a tender heart.

❧ Discussion Questions ❧

1. What is the best compliment you've ever received?
   What effect did it have on you?

2. What is the worst insult or most hurtful comment
   someone has said about you? How did it affect you?

3. On a scale of one to ten, how resilient do you think you
   are to criticism? Do you bounce back quickly, or do you
   withdraw?

4. What's the difference between helpful advice and criticism? What advice have you received that was hard to hear but ultimately proved beneficial? What lessons did this experience teach you about how to be a valuable advisor to your friends?

5. What verse from Scripture makes you feel close to God and loved by Him? Why?

6. Are you careful about taking people's words to heart? Do you place equal value on everyone's opinion, or do you take into account each person's character, how close you are, and whether you trust and respect the person?

Kindness

 All around you, people are feeling lonely, invisible, and insignificant. Be the girl who takes a genuine interest in others. Spread kindness, love, and compassion.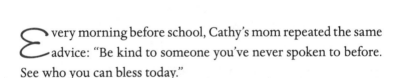

Every morning before school, Cathy's mom repeated the same advice: "Be kind to someone you've never spoken to before. See who you can bless today."

Cathy and her sister would look at each other and try not to roll their eyes because their mother—well, she treated this advice as if it might cure cancer. She said it with an excited gleam in her eye and her most joyful voice.

And when the girls came home from school, their mother always followed up. She'd grin and ask the million-dollar question.

"So, who did you choose to bless today?"

Cathy and her sister had inside jokes about their mother's quest to bless. Being friendly came naturally to her because she was an extrovert.

It was no surprise that people *loved* her. She made friends wherever she went, chatting up the bagger at the supermarket, the custodian at the girls' school, and anyone who crossed her path.

Sometimes people would spill their life story. They'd get teary-eyed and say things like, "It feels really good to talk about this. Nobody has ever asked me."

Their mother would cry, too, and always end with an encouraging word. And though her love for people and impromptu conversations could annoy the girls—especially when the sob stories came—they admired their mom's patience and genuine interest in others.

Since Cathy was shy, she felt awkward taking her mom's advice. But after practicing on the cafeteria workers at school and a girl in algebra, Cathy's motivation grew. She started talking to people who stood alone during break. She figured they might need a friend.

Finding someone new to bless each day actually brought Cathy out of her shell. It also revealed the power of words. Even a simple statement like "Hey, Bess! Congrats on making the tennis team!" could prompt a big smile. Seeing how people lit up inspired Cathy to keep being kind and seeing who she could bless.

Over time, Cathy and her sister grew braver. They even chose to be kind and friendly to people who weren't kind and friendly back.

This led to a new inside joke where Cathy and her sister would say, "One day we'll crack them! One day we'll get a smile!"

Their mother advised them to not take it personally if someone didn't respond warmly because they didn't know what difficult circumstances that person might be battling.

Their mom knew about battles because she was battling cancer. And when that cancer took her life, it rocked their family and the entire community.

After her mom's death, Cathy experienced a dark and terrible time, yet she clearly saw how *deeply* people mourned her mother. It wasn't just that she'd died too young; it was that people couldn't imagine living in a world without her.

The funeral was packed, and the audience was diverse. There were wealthy people, poor people, whites, African-Americans, Latinos, adults, and children. Many of the faces there surprised Cathy—like the teller from the bank, the man who painted their home, and their postal carrier.

The grief in the church was palpable, and for hours after the service, people with deeply sorrowful eyes approached Cathy and her family and shared story after story. One woman even said, "When I was in a homeless shelter, your mom taught me life skills. She taught me to believe in myself. She helped me get a job."

People choked up and cried as they talked about her mom. As Cathy consoled these strangers whose lives her mother had touched, she found herself wishing she'd known, while her mom was alive, how much people loved and respected her.

To Cathy, she was just Mom, the woman who hounded her about brushing her teeth and blessing someone new each day. But to the world she was an angel, always appearing out of nowhere to help someone down on their luck, down on themselves, or down on life.

Though losing her mom was a tragedy, it was also a wake-up call for Cathy. It forced her to face the reality that death is a part of life and that living well means loving well.

Her mom had often said that people are hungry to be noticed, loved, and heard. After witnessing the heartfelt reactions to her mother's death, Cathy knew her mom was right.

Cancer took her mom too soon, but not before she had led a meaningful life. More than anything, Cathy wanted to live a meaningful life as well. Inspired by her mother, Cathy wanted to leave a legacy of kindness that impacted everyone she encountered.

········•·····•······•·····•······· ♥ ·······•·· ·······••·····•···•··

"A new command I give you: Love
one another. As I have loved you, so
you must love one another."

—JOHN 13:34

··•·······•··•······•·•··•······•••··········••···•···•••···••···•····•·· ··

Be the Blessing

In any relationship, the natural tendency is to focus inward. You probably think a lot about how other people make you feel and whether you feel accepted or rejected, loved or overlooked.

Your feelings have great merit, and it's important to notice them and figure out what they are telling you. Tuning into the emotions that people trigger in you—good or bad—can provide major clues to help you determine which relationships are healthy and beneficial and which ones are not.

But as you pay attention to how *you* feel, you may forget to consider how *other people* feel. You may get so wrapped up in your emotions that you don't stop to think about the emotions getting triggered in others.

This tendency we all have leads to self-centered thinking and relationship problems. It makes people feel disconnected and alone even in a group. When everyone focuses inward, connections can't form. Nobody feels important or significant because nobody is reaching out.

I once received an e-mail from a woman who leads a Bible study for teen girls. She said that in private conversations with her, many girls complained about feeling *invisible* when they were in a group.

Unfortunately, this dynamic is common today. With everyone

fixated on self-promotion, our society has grown increasingly ego-centric. The result is isolation or, at best, poor relationships.

The remedy, I believe, is to look outward, notice the needs of others, and make deliberate efforts to help people feel valued. To do this, you'll have to put your phone down and really talk with people.

We all know what it's like to feel invisible, don't we? We've all been in that awkward situation where we've been ignored or dismissed.

Maybe you felt invisible standing in a circle of girls who kept bragging about the concert they attended last night. It's fine they didn't invite you, but do they have to rub it in?

Maybe you felt invisible when a girl talking to you stopped mid-sentence, waved to someone, and ditched you to chase after her.

Maybe you felt invisible spending three hours at a party where nobody cared that you came. If you hadn't shown up, nobody would have noticed.

Now let's consider this from a different perspective. Think about the times that you—consciously or not—may have made other people feel invisible.

Maybe you and your friends made dinner plans without inviting the girl who was standing right next to you.

Maybe someone smiled at you in the hall, and you responded with a blank stare.

Maybe you've ignored the girl who eats lunch alone every day, purposely avoiding her eyes so you don't feel guilty about passing her by.

The point is, all of us feel invisible sometimes. And all of us sometimes make others feel invisible too.

Once you can admit this, you're ready to move forward. You're ready to be the girl who God calls you to be, a girl who can take the love He generously gives you and freely share it with others.

That's how God's love works, after all. We love because God loved us first (1 John 4:19). So instead of praying for God to bless you, pray to *be* a blessing to others. Imagine being the answer to someone's prayer, a prayer that only God has heard and one that He's chosen to answer by using you to show His love.

························ ♥ ·······························

Let us not become weary in doing
good, for at the proper time we will reap
a harvest if we do not give up.

—GALATIANS 6:9

···

Who Needs Comfort Today?

While driving to school each morning, my girls and I pray in the car. One thing we ask God to do is open our eyes to the people around us who may be suffering. I want us to notice the ones who need extra love and encouragement.

It isn't always obvious when someone is struggling or facing tough times. You can't always tell when a heart has been hurt or shattered. After all, people in pain don't normally curl up and cry in public. They face the day like anyone else does, sometimes hiding behind a bright smile and a good attitude.

There are also times when pain gets played out as anger or a tough act. School bullies, for instance, have probably experienced pain that hardened them. Rather than deal with their pain, they dump it on others.

And this is one reason why God calls you and me to love and pray for our enemies (Matthew 5:44). Only love can break the cycle of hurt. Only love can soften a hardened heart.

God's love enables us to extend grace to others. We need His help because we all jump to conclusions about people and, based on very limited details, often assume the worst. I'm convinced that if we could see people through God's eyes and hear the prayers He hears, we'd be much kinder and more compassionate. We would approach other people with a softer heart and a stronger resolve to be a friend and a peacemaker.

The opportunities to be a friend and a peacemaker are endless! All around us, every day, people need comfort and companionship. So when your heart feels tugged to do good—to call an old friend or thank a former teacher for encouraging you to chase a dream that became a reality for you—that's God at work. That is God speaking to you through the Holy Spirit, prompting you to act on His behalf.

God isn't going to call your friend directly, but you can. God won't be visiting your teacher in her classroom, but you can.

It's truly awesome to think about how perfect God's timing is. Since He knows everything about everyone, He knows exactly when to plant those urges in you.

This is why your friend may say, "I'm *so* glad you called. I really needed this talk." It's why your teacher may get emotional as you thank her for her impact on you. After a tough week of teaching, you reminded her why she loves her job.

Sometimes, unfortunately, your kindness won't be well-received. When this happens, you can't take it personally, just as Cathy's mom mentioned in the opening story. You never know what battles others are facing or what kind of day they've had, so rather than be offended, just say a quick prayer for these people and let it go.

Even if people don't appreciate your kind acts, God does. He sees them, and He is pleased. Nothing you do out of love is a waste, and when you love with a pure heart, expecting nothing in return, you are embodying the Spirit of Christ. You are showing the world what it means to love people with no strings attached.

All around you, there are people who long to be seen. They want a reminder that somebody cares. Taking one minute to bless an individual can leave a deep impression. God may use you to give encouragement to someone running low on hope.

God puts people in your path for a reason, so open your eyes and your heart to them. Listen to what He tells you. Trust those nudges from the Holy Spirit, and choose to bless others.

······•·······•·····•······•···•······ ♥ ·····•··•···•·····•··•···•···•····•····

All around you, there are people who long to be seen. They want a reminder that somebody cares.

··•·······•·•······•··•·•······•·•·····•···•····•··•···•····•·•·······•·•·····•····

Taking a Genuine Interest in People

People often ask each other, "How are you doing?"

And though this sounds like an invitation to open up, it's really a courtesy. A greeting. A gateway to small talk.

When someone asks, "How are you doing?" they aren't looking for an elaborate answer. Typically they expect a generic response that goes down easy and won't create awkward silences. Something like "I'm great, thanks. How are you?"

But not every day is great. Sometimes we have problems and issues we need to talk through and think through. Finding a safe place to share them isn't easy because not everyone is willing to listen.

Why? Because people are busy. We often don't have the time or don't want to make the time to care. Sometimes we'd rather not know about a person's problems because then we'd feel obligated to help, and we've got enough problems of our own already.

For whatever reason, we often keep people's pain at a distance. Instead of leaning in to listen, we draw back. We stick with easy conversations that keep things simple and convenient.

But God created all of us for more than simple and convenient. He wants our hearts to grow and stretch with love and compassion.

Hearing someone's story—the *real* story—can help you as much as it helps the person telling it. Hearing another person's struggles forces you out of your comfort zone and builds empathy as you learn what challenges he or she is dealing with.

Listening can also prepare you for the future. What your friend faces today may be similar to a situation you'll face down the road. As you listen to her talk, you can think about what you would do if you were in her position. Her story plants seeds that may help you deal wisely with something in your future or the future of someone you love.

I once heard about a father who took great interest in his teenage daughter's life. He wanted to know everything she was going through, the good and the bad. And when they had one-on-one time, he liked to ask a question that led to rich and interesting dialogue.

"So, what's it like to be you today?"

Imagine being asked that question by someone you deeply trust. Imagine the freedom of taking a deep breath and feeling comfortable enough to honestly reply.

You really want to know? Here's what it's like to be me right now. My favorite aunt has cancer. My best friend is moving. My sister borrowed my favorite shirt and ruined it, and she isn't even sorry.

My mom yells at my dad. My brother is a superstar who everybody loves—but I hate him because he steals all the attention. To top it off, I got a C on my world history test, and I have a crush on a boy who called me the wrong name when I passed him in the hall. Nobody knows what it's like to be me because nobody is me.

It drives me crazy, you know? I can't find a single person who understands me the way I want to be understood. It makes me want to jump out of my skin. It makes me wish I could be someone else.

I'm sorry to dump this on you, but it feels good to say it out loud. I don't trust anyone enough to share how I'm really feeling, so I bottle it all up and pretend I'm fine. But I'm not fine. I feel like I could explode. Right now, it really hurts to be me.

Conversations like this are therapeutic and healing. They offer deep insight into a person's heart and mind. Unfortunately, they don't happen enough because rarely do any of us feel safe enough to be so raw and honest. We're scared to take the risk.

But when you avoid all risks in your relationships, you miss opportunities to connect in significant, life-giving ways. You miss hearing someone say, "Me too. I thought I was the only one!" You miss having the chance to comfort people by looking them in the eyes and saying what they long to hear.

I'm so sorry. You've got a lot on you, and I'm glad you trusted me enough to share it. I won't tell anyone. And if it makes you feel better, I get it. Some days I want to jump out of my skin too. You're not the only one to feel that way. But now that we know we both have rough days, maybe we can be there for each other at least to listen.

It's okay if you don't have the perfect words or the right solution for someone's problem. It's okay if all you can offer is a listening ear because that's usually what people want most.

And when someone's problems are bigger than you can handle, you can point them to someone better equipped to help: a school counselor, his or her parents, or a trusted adult. You can guide the friend with love and discretion so that little problems don't become big problems.

································ ♥ ································

You must all be quick to listen, slow to speak, and slow to get angry.

—JAMES 1:19 NLT

··

Finding Opportunities to Bless Others

Taking a genuine interest in people means more than simply smiling a lot and saying, "How are you doing?" It calls you to look past labels and appearances and have a healthy curiosity about the people you encounter.

It also means wanting to know their *real* stories and being a good listener.

Imagine how different your life would be if you looked at the classmates you pass in the halls every day and wondered:

♡ *What are their dreams?*
♡ *What holds them back from those dreams?*
♡ *How can I help them?*
♡ *What can I learn from them?*
♡ *How might God be weaving our stories together?*

Showing interest in your friends is important, but that's a given. Your friends expect you to care about them, right?

But showing kindness and compassion to people you don't know well catches them off guard. It sends them a clear and welcome message that they aren't invisible. To be noticed and loved by someone who has no obligation to acknowledge you or love you is extremely powerful.

All around you, every day, God gives you opportunities to be a blessing like that. Pray to have your eyes open so you can recognize those opportunities and help the people around you feel less lonely, invisible, or insignificant.

With each life you bless, God blesses your life with richness, significance, and joy.

···•···••••··•••···••··•••···••··••••··· ♥ ···••···••···••••··••···••••··•••••··•··

"Just say what God tells you at that time, for it is not you who will be speaking, but the Holy Spirit."

—MARK 13:11 NLT

··•···••••··•••···••··•••····••··•••···••··•••····•••··••···••••··•••···••••··•··

❥ Discussion Questions ❦

1. Think of a time when you felt lonely, invisible, or insignificant. Did the experience soften your heart or harden it? Why?

2. Tell about a time you hurt someone by forgetting to consider his or her feelings. What did you learn?

3. What can girls do to become more outwardly focused in group settings? What are some things you can do to help other people feel visible?

4. Think of a time when the Holy Spirit nudged you to do a special act of kindness. Did you act on that nudge? Why or why not?

5. On a scale of one to ten, how well do you listen? Do people seem to feel safe opening up to you?

6. What are some differences between showing love to a friend and showing love to a person you barely know? Which one is harder for you? Why?

4

Character

Through technology, you speak to an
audience. Use your voice for good.
Be an encourager, not a critic.

It all started at a sleepover with some girls whom Chloe loosely
called friends.

She used the term *loosely* because they could be really mean at
times, even to one another.

Earlier that night, they'd gone to the high school football game.
While waiting in line for a Coke, someone snapped pictures of two
girls wearing the same dress. One girl was tall and thin; the other
was short and stocky. Chloe thought they both looked cute, just
different.

"Let's create an anonymous Twitter account," suggested
Elizabeth, the sleepover host. "We can be the school gossip and
call people out on their fashion disasters."

The girls agreed this would be fun, but it had to stay anonymous. That way they wouldn't get in trouble.

For the first post, they did a side-by-side collage of the girls
in identical dresses. They wrote: *Fashion Patrol Survey: Who wore*

it better? Laughter filled the room as they tweeted the post and launched their online identity.

In the weeks that followed, their Twitter account gained followers. It created buzz at school as people wondered who was behind @MVHSGossip and followed the account. As their audience grew, so did their retweets. People began messaging them with juicy new developments.

One tweet that took off was a picture of the head cheerleader's father on the side of the road getting arrested for drunk driving. Since the cheerleader was a goody-goody, people loved it. The picture got thirty-four retweets, which told the girls they were on to something good.

This is when their strategy evolved. Instead of just gossiping, they would now capture embarrassing moments. Parties were prime opportunities to catch people with their guards down, but they had to be careful not to be seen taking the pictures they posted.

Chloe definitely didn't like where this Twitter account was headed. It made her feel very uncomfortable. It was bad enough for these girls to publicize every wrong move people made, but to start rumors about a freshman girl going to Weight Watchers or fabricate stories about the track coach having marital problems? What was the point of being so cruel?

Now every tweet from @MVHSGossip was an attempt to bring somebody down. And though Chloe never posted anything, she felt guilty by association.

Chloe felt completely helpless to stop this smear campaign because she didn't want to get on these girls' bad side. She didn't want to be the subject of one of their cruel, demeaning tweets. Given their lack of conscience, she was certain that they'd turn on her in a heartbeat.

It didn't seem like a big deal when they started the account, but now it felt terribly wrong. Chloe seriously regretted her involvement, and the longer this account went on, the worse she felt.

················· ♥ ·················

> "A tree is identified by its fruit. If a tree is good, its fruit will be good. If a tree is bad, its fruit will be bad."
>
> **—MATTHEW 12:33** NLT

················· ·················

It's Your Microphone—How Will You Use It?

Imagine yourself at a school assembly, standing on stage before six hundred people. The principal has handed you a microphone and invited you to share an important message.

All eyes in the auditorium are on you. You're nervous and excited, unsure about being in the spotlight like this. Do you love it or hate it? Will you impress your classmates or go down as a joke?

Since you've never been onstage before, you have everyone's full attention. They're wondering if you have anything relevant to say.

Do well, and your classmates will listen again next time. Blow this chance, and they may tune you out forever.

It's a lot of pressure to speak in front of a crowd this size. You choose your words carefully because your name and your reputation are at stake.

Now apply this analogy to social media. Take a minute to think about what you share on Instagram or other social networks. Are the words you use online the same words you would say out loud? Would you read your typed words and verbally share your online opinions while standing in front of an auditorium full of people?

Being on social media is like being on stage with a microphone. It's a platform that allows you to speak to hundreds or thousands of people at once, depending on the size of your following.

Just as you wouldn't stand on stage and blurt out random thoughts, angry rants, or humiliating remarks, you should avoid these kinds of posts on social media. You'd be wise to remember how everything you post—even on Snapchat—becomes part of your online record.

This record may not mean much now, but it will eventually. It may either open doors or slam doors in your face in the near future as you apply for college, try to join a sorority, go out for team sports, seek membership in prestigious organizations, and interview for jobs.

In this day and age, people *will* Google your name before accepting you into their group. They'll make assumptions about your character based on the choices you've made with technology—or the choices your friends have made for you on social media.

Imagine being rejected from your dream job because at age thirteen you shared a questionable picture.

Imagine losing a scholarship because your anonymous Twitter account (like the one in the opening story) came to light as lies usually do, costing you all credibility and respect.

Something that seems like harmless fun can put your reputation as well as your future opportunities at risk. It's not worth making these avoidable mistakes. It isn't smart to share in a public forum every thought, mood, and feeling you have with no regard for the consequences.

A lot of people approach the Internet with an "anything goes" attitude, but I challenge you to aim higher. I encourage you to set standards for yourself and be as intentional online as you would be on stage.

One benefit of technology—when it's used wisely—is that it

allows you to reach a large audience. It gives you a microphone to project your voice far and wide.

This is a powerful gift, my friend! This is a tool you can use to impact your generation and enrich lives.

God created you specifically for this digital age. He puts messages on your heart that your peers need to hear, messages that might turn someone's day or life around. Through technology, you can communicate quickly, efficiently, and cheaply. You can be a messenger with a special mission and a God-given purpose.

Our world looks at social media as a way to get famous, get even, and get attention. But more importantly, social media presents an opportunity to do good. Only God knows the countless number of lives you can ultimately impact—and in a small window of time.

So embrace the potential of technology. Share things worth reading. Earn your audience's trust by being the kind of girl who people *want* to listen to.

❤

Are the words you use online the same words you would say out loud?

Be an Encourager

Do you know anyone who sees the best in you and always points it out?

Although she may notice your flaws and imperfections, she focuses on the good. She sees more potential in you than you see in yourself. And when your spirits are down, she boosts you up. Her words fill your heart with peace, hope, and joy.

Girls like this are called *encouragers*. They understand the realities of our broken world. They're aware of people's short-comings. Yet instead of dwelling on what's wrong, they magnify what's right. They are change agents who build people up instead of tearing them down.

An encourager will:

♡ Speak kind thoughts like "I love that shirt on you. Red is your color!"
♡ Start good conversations and turn bad ones around.
♡ See people through God's eyes.
♡ Speak the truth in love. An encourager loves sharing fun truths (like telling her best friend she's beautiful) and is careful when sharing hard truths (like telling her best friend that her boyfriend is a liar, and she has proof). She prays for wisdom before addressing hard issues.
♡ Comfort those who just blew it, remembering how a word of encouragement during a failure is worth more than an hour of praise after success.
♡ Give compliments freely, not to butter people up for future favors, but because it feels good. Her heart and motives are pure.
♡ Learn to control negative feelings like anger and jealousy so they don't control her.
♡ Radiate a light that makes people naturally crave her company.

The opposite of an encourager is a critic. We all know critics, right? Unfortunately, technology makes criticism easier than ever. People feel anonymous as they hide behind their screens, and as their fingers jump ahead of their brains, keyboard courage takes over.

Keyboard courage is when you type things that you'd never

say to someone's face. You get brazen and bold because you can't see the damage you're doing.

When you speak in person, you witness the impact of your words. You know you've crossed a line when your remark causes a shocked reaction on someone's face or tears in another person's eyes.

But with technology you don't have that instant feedback. With a screen between you and the receiver, you may not stop at just one irresponsible remark. There are no visual cues to alert you to the damage you're doing and the fact that you should stop immediately.

Critics bring people down. They pollute the air for everyone and easily create a hostile, even toxic, atmosphere.

A critic will:

- Nitpick every detail that's wrong.
- Chronically complain.
- Always have a score to settle or a bone to pick.
- Freely criticize, but get defensive when he or she is the target.
- Express every negative thought, even irrelevant ones.
- Struggle to see the good.
- Take a good conversation down a negative road.
- Kick people when they're down.
- Kick people when they're up.
- Stir the pot of drama and gossip.
- Have no social filter.
- Have no true friends.
- Be hard to tolerate, which leads to an empty and lonely life.

Many critics believe they're helpful. They pride themselves on being the mouthpiece of what other people think but are too scared to say.

Critics might look at an encourager and think, *Ugh! She's annoying. She's too syrupy-sweet. I'm gonna be real. I'll tell it like it is. No sugarcoating the truth over here!*

What these critics don't realize is how off-putting their negativity is. They speak with no grace, no hope, no love, and no tact. And while they can build a cult following by being funny and making people laugh, the fans they attract tend to be just as snarky as they are.

Is it likely that a critic's fan base will stick around for long? Will they be loyal?

Of course not. Eventually those fans will leave. They'll either turn on the critic or move on to the next cutup who is funnier and more entertaining.

I imagine that life gets very lonely for critics who hit rock bottom and have nobody to turn to. I imagine that regret must really kick in when their mean behavior no longer pays off.

Counselors say it takes about five compliments to counterbalance every criticism.[2] And when you consider the deep damage that critics can cause, it becomes clear why the world needs more encouragers. So choose your words carefully online and in real life. Don't stomp on anyone's heart.

How you treat people online influences the way they treat you. Just as critics attract critics, encouragers attract encouragers. And when encouragers sit in your social media audience, they'll drown out the naysayers. They'll stick up for you when critics speak. They won't be threatened by any success you have because they're smart enough to understand that you don't have to fail for them to succeed.

Our world is hungry for inspiration. People want a break from pollution on the Internet. So be an encourager who builds community, not a critic who breaks spirits. Use your voice for good, and you'll see other encouragers rally around you.

························· ♥ ·······························

The words of the reckless pierce like swords,
but the tongue of the wise brings healing.
—PROVERBS 12:18

···

Twenty Tips for Positive Social Media Habits

Being smart with technology is really a matter of being conscientious. Before you post or share, think through the message and possible consequences. Ask yourself if your words are a wise use of the public stage and your microphone.

Here are twenty tips to help you decide what you should share online. By practicing these habits, you'll learn to use your microphone for good.

1. Pick a goal that pleases God. Social media should be used to spread love, not poison. Look for what is good, right, praiseworthy, and admirable in this world, and then talk about those things (Philippians 4:8).

2. Know your followers. Stranger danger is very real online because people can stalk you without your knowledge and pretend to be someone they're not. The Internet is packed with predators, trolls, and people who take advantage of beautiful young girls like you. *Be vigilant about who you let follow you.*

Keep your accounts private, and if you don't know the person asking, decline the request to follow you. If someone looks questionable, has no identifying pictures, uses an anonymous name, or posts anything inappropriate, block that person. If someone bullies you or writes mean-spirited comments, block that account as well. Embrace an online policy of "One strike and you're out."

Above all, pray for wisdom. Ask God to help you discern who you should and shouldn't interact with on social media so you can enjoy it while keeping yourself safe (Matthew 10:16).

3. Before you post, consider three questions: *Is it kind? Is it true? Is it necessary?* The key word here is *necessary*. While it may be true that your friend looks super-skinny in her photo, is it necessary to post *#eataburger*? Are put-downs that masquerade as praise ever helpful?

4. Before you share online, imagine answering the question, *Are you sure?* Whenever you delete a social media post or a picture from your phone, you're typically asked a question like "Are you sure you want to delete this?"

The purpose is to make you pause and think. And while you usually see this question *after* you've posted, it's really needed *before* you post.

How many social media train wrecks could be prevented if people took the time to ask themselves, *Am I sure I want to post this?* before they shared pictures and thoughts online?

This reminder doesn't exist, of course, but you can still use this question as a litmus test before you share anything. And if you're at all unsure, don't post it. Chances are, your gut instinct is warning you that posting is a bad idea (Ephesians 5:10).

5. If you aren't feeling the love, stay off social media.
We all get in bad moods, fly off the handle, and overreact at times.

But giving your emotional monster a keypad may lead to trouble. You're likely to share something you'll later regret.

So before going online, be sure your head and heart are in the right place. Cool off from any anger, jealousy, or frustration you're feeling so you can act intentionally, not impulsively (Ephesians 4:26). The Internet isn't a dumping ground. It's also not the place to vent, air dirty laundry, or call your best friend out for a lie she told.

6. Keep a thick skin and a tender heart. Put on your armor because people can be mean and social media trolling is rampant (Ephesians 6:10–18). Even if you're not blatantly attacked, you may be the target of a snarky comment or unfavorable post.

Prepare in advance for potential meanness. Remember that knowing who you are in Christ can soften the blow of negativity and keep it from hardening your heart.

7. Learn from your mistakes—and the mistakes others make. It only takes three seconds of poor judgment to set an online wrecking ball in motion. Every day, teens make life-altering mistakes that hurt them, their peers, and their families.

Most mistakes are caused by not thinking through the possible consequences. Every social media choice you make has a consequence (Galatians 6:7). Everything you share—even a private text or a Snapchat message to one person you trust—can potentially go viral and be seen by thousands or even millions of people. One quick screenshot of your message or photo can jump-start a disaster.

We all make mistakes, but online mistakes can lead to public humiliation. Please don't repeat the mistakes that you see making headlines today. Don't share anything, even with your best friend, that you'd be mortified to see splashed across the front page of a newspaper.

8. Make sure you're emotionally ready for social media. It's normal to feel left out, jealous, or insecure when you see your friends on Instagram getting frozen yogurt without you, having fun at the lake, or looking so gorgeous that you feel like a monkey in comparison.

But if you dwell on these negative feelings or fall to pieces every time you're not included, you are *not* emotionally ready to be on social media.

Social media is meant to be fun. It's a quick and easy way to stay connected. And if scrolling through a newsfeed causes you more heartache than pleasure, sign off or delete the app. Take your feelings as a sign that the best moments of other people's lives are blinding you to your personal blessings, and it's time to pull back.

Envy can eat you up (Proverbs 14:30). So before you join a social media community, ask yourself, *Do I bounce back quickly when I see I wasn't invited someplace? Do I constantly want to trade lives with the people I follow? Can I learn to be happy for them and grateful for my life?* If social media triggers sadness and envy, it's best to stay off.

9. Pay attention to the conversations you start. Jesus said we can identify a tree by the fruit it produces (Matthew 12:33). And if you want to know if your social media habits honor Him, look at the reactions people have to what you say. What fruit do your posts produce?

Do your posts trigger kind comments, or do they trigger gossip? Do they bring out the best in people, or do they bring out their dark, snarky, and sarcastic side?

The responses people have to the things you share are telling. While their reactions can't present a complete picture, they do offer clues about whether you're using your microphone responsibly.

10. Build up your friends, family, and classmates. If someone has ever written a special post about you—perhaps on your birthday—you know how awesome it makes you feel. So look for opportunities to celebrate others and shine a spotlight on them (1 Thessalonians 5:11).

If your friend plays volleyball, for instance, talk about what an inspiration she is and how proud you are when she nails a hit. If your mom is a fantastic cook, show a feast she made for your family and mention how the smell of dinner in the oven makes you feel loved. If a girl in your drama class is making cool headbands, share a picture and brag about her talent.

Building up the people around you benefits them and you. It boosts their confidence and makes you the encourager that God wants you to be.

11. Recognize what is and what isn't your story to tell. When something wonderful or terrible happens to someone close to you, you may want to share it. Whether it's a celebration or a need for prayer, you may want all your social media followers to know.

Before you post, however, check with the person. Make sure he or she is okay with your sharing the news. If your friend was just chosen for the lead role in the school play, for instance, let her break the story. Let her surprise people and enjoy that initial excitement.

On the same note, if your friend's father is ill and headed to the hospital, let her family decide whether to announce it publicly. Some people are private and don't want personal details known, even to ask for prayers.

Honor your friends by letting them tell their stories and making sure that any updates you post have their approval (Luke 6:31).

12. Avoid apps that allow anonymity and promote secrecy. Anonymous postings bring out the haters, and nothing good comes from spending time in secretive forums. You ask for trouble when you use apps that allow you to hide things (e.g. photos and texts) from your parents or conceal your identity.

Everything you do on your digital device should be done "in the light" (1 John 1:7). You should have nothing to hide or be ashamed of. If you feel compelled to hide your posts or be sneaky and secretive, that's a sign you're misusing technology.

13. Limit selfies. In 2013, Oxford Dictionaries named *selfie* the word of the year because use of the word grew 117 percent in that period.[3]

Selfies can be fun, but their popularity shows how all-about-me our society has become. Instead of living God-centered lives, we're living me-centered lives, and our culture supports us every step of the way.

Your pictures tell your story. And if you're always posting selfies—well, that tells people your life is all about you. Is that really the story you want to tell?

Girls often use selfies to fish for compliments or be affirmed for their beauty, but I encourage you to aim higher. Keep selfies to a minimum, and make your posts more about your spirit and less about how your hair looks today (Colossians 3:2).

14. Detach from your numbers. Social media has made popularity quantifiable. Among your peers, the barometer often used to measure your importance and worth is how many "likes," followers, and shares you get.

But numbers alone can be misleading. What gets liked and applauded online isn't always important to God. For the full picture, you must measure the numbers against His truths.

After all, Jesus Christ had twelve active followers while He was on earth. Adolf Hitler had millions. These numbers show the difference between what's good and what's popular.

God doesn't care if you have three followers or three thousand followers, two "likes" or two hundred "likes." He simply wants you to light up your corner of the universe. The size of your audience is irrelevant because drawing even *one heart* closer to God is far more valuable than racking up fifty thousand "likes" on a picture.

Our world is obsessed with numbers, but you don't have to be. You don't have to feel "less than" the most popular girls online. In the grand scheme of life, social media numbers are meaningless. Your posts can be deleted with the swipe of a finger and forgotten in a flash.

So keep your eyes on God. Let His praise satisfy your need for recognition and attention (John 12:43).

15. Don't base your confidence and sense of value on social media. If you rely on social media to build you up, you also give it power to break you down. Social media can mess with your mind, your emotions, and your self-confidence.

In two days you can go from thinking *Everybody loves me* to *Everybody is against me* because your friend Amy liked Holly's picture from the beach and not yours and then your tennis team forgot to tag you in a post.

While social media is a fun way to connect with friends, letting it dictate your mood gives it a power it shouldn't have in anyone's life. Enjoy social media as an "extra," but don't base your confidence or sense of value on it. Put your faith in things that are real and reliable so your emotions stay off the roller coaster (Jeremiah 17:7).

16. Set high standards for yourself. In today's virtual world, there's a reckless disregard for content. Many people post pictures and comments that are rude, racy, and completely inappropriate. Low standards of what is acceptable lead to online bullying, tarnished reputations, and other social media nightmares.

Please don't get caught in that trap. Set a high bar for everything you post even if the people around you don't. Be a responsible digital citizen—and remember that what you put online creates a digital record attached to your name.

Whatever online reputation you create for yourself today will affect the way people perceive you and receive you today, tomorrow, and for many years into the future (1 Peter 3:16).

17. Carefully inspect pictures before you share them.
A friend of mine who mentors teenage girls once received a text from a girl trying on prom dresses. She wanted my friend's opinion on a dress. My friend told her, "That dress looks great on you, but please delete this picture from your phone because in the dressing room mirror, I see a reflection of your friend in her bra and underwear."

Technology makes it easy to both intentionally and accidentally capture people in compromising positions. So before you post an image, study it. *Make sure everyone in the shot—not just you—looks okay.*

And if someone dislikes the way she looks or asks you to take down an embarrassing picture, respect her feelings. Don't make anyone look bad by sharing an unflattering image (Romans 12:10).

18. Don't spend so much time in the online world that you neglect the real world. The best moments happen face-to-face (Matthew 18:20). So put your phone down when you're with your family and friends so you can enjoy the kind of deep, meaningful conversations you simply can't have online.

19. Settle conflicts in person. When you and a friend have an issue, try to talk in person or call her instead of sending texts. Arguments can escalate quickly through technology, and messages often get interpreted the wrong way. This creates tension in relationships that may be hard to recover from.

Rather than take that risk, make an effort to see your friend or pick up the phone and call her (Ephesians 4:26). Doing one or the other will show respect for her as well as your maturity and your concern for the friendship.

20. Be a class act. God gave you a voice to encourage people. Through your social media microphone, you can empower many people at once.

So put your energy, intelligence, and zest for life to good use. Drown out the voices of the critics by being a voice of love, grace, and wisdom. Invite your friends to do the same.

The more people you inspire to use their microphone for good, the less the critics get heard. And once you shut out the critics, real progress can begin.

❤

If scrolling through a newsfeed causes
you more heartache than pleasure,
sign off or delete the app.

The Gift of Your Voice

When my aunt lost her husband to cancer, she learned something about the power of words.

My uncle passed away peacefully at home with his family

around his bedside. As you'd imagine, there were many tears cried and many words of love spoken.

The nurses from hospice told my aunt that hearing is the last sense to go. They encouraged the family to keep talking even if my uncle's eyes were closed and he appeared to be unconscious.

"So we kept talking and talking as if he could hear us," my aunt later told me. "We were still talking as he left this world."

I'd like you to take a minute and think about this: of all the senses that humans possess, hearing is the last one to go.[4] Even in our final moments on earth, when our bodies shut down and our minds drift away, we may still have the capacity to hear words being spoken.

If that doesn't testify to the power of words, what does?

My friend, your voice is a gift from God. It empowers you to be an instrument of His love. Like any gift from God, you can use it the way He intended—to produce good—or you can use it to cause harm (Proverbs 18:21).

My hope and prayer is that you'll use your voice wisely both in person and online. I hope you make it your goal to speak the truth in love.

If your words can comfort people as they take their last breaths on earth, imagine what they might do for people who are alive and fully alert. Imagine how deeply your words might register in a mind that is fully conscious.

Through technology, your words can reach many people at once. You can connect with friends, share ideas, and build community. God created you for this moment in time, and your gift back to Him is to be a good steward of the digital innovations that are shaping and changing the way your generation communicates.

Our world needs more encouragers. Will you step up? You have the opportunity to use the Internet to be a positive voice to your peers. So share words and ideas that build people up, inspire them, and make them want to tune in again the next time you take the microphone.

♥

The wise are known for their understanding,
and pleasant words are persuasive.

—PROVERBS 16:21 NLT

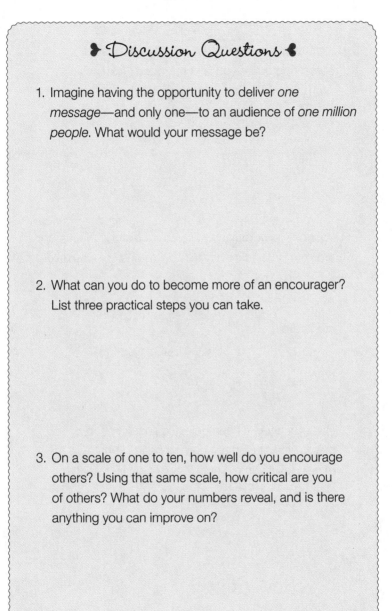

❧ Discussion Questions ❧

1. Imagine having the opportunity to deliver *one message*—and only one—to an audience of *one million people*. What would your message be?

2. What can you do to become more of an encourager? List three practical steps you can take.

3. On a scale of one to ten, how well do you encourage others? Using that same scale, how critical are you of others? What do your numbers reveal, and is there anything you can improve on?

4. Have you ever sent a text message or posted something online you later regretted? If so, what prompted your change of heart?

5. Your online words and pictures tell a story. What story are your posts currently telling? What story would you like them to tell?

6. Have you ever felt compelled to share a special message that God put on your heart? What was the message? If you did post it, how did you feel after sharing it?

5

Commitment

There's a difference between
online friends and real friends.
 Online friends take two seconds to
"like" your latest post. Real friends
take off an afternoon to visit you
when you need them most.

It was supposed to be a fun day of brother-sister bonding. Daniel and Paige started their adventure with a trip to the tackle store to buy bait, hooks, and a fishing rod for Paige.

They were headed to the river when Daniel received a text. His girlfriend was asking about their dinner plans. Using one hand to steer the truck, Daniel picked up his phone with the other and texted her back.

Paige saw the stop sign as they approached it, and she assumed Daniel saw it too. But, distracted, he whizzed past it and into the intersection. Paige glanced around for cops, afraid that Daniel might get a ticket, but what caught her eye instead was a blue Ford Taurus headed straight toward her.

A split second later, the two cars collided. Sounds of shattered glass, screeching brakes, and crushed metal filled Paige's ears as the Taurus hit her side of Daniel's truck.

The accident happened suddenly and without warning, and as witnesses rushed over to help them and call an ambulance, all Paige could think about was the throbbing pain in her right leg.

Although Paige was wearing her seatbelt, the impact on her side of the car led to serious injuries—a compound femur fracture and a lacerated spleen. Her injuries would heal with time, but she needed surgery on her leg. Doctors said she wouldn't play soccer for several months.

Daniel felt so guilty, especially since his injuries were minor, but Paige wasn't angry. She told Daniel to quit beating himself up because the outcome could have been far worse.

To prepare for surgery, Paige spent several days in a hospital bed with her leg elevated in a traction splint. All she could do was watch television and talk.

On Instagram, Snapchat, and Facebook, Paige asked her friends to pray for a successful surgery. She received an outpouring of love and support that boosted her spirits.

But what hurt Paige's feelings was the lack of visitors she had. Family members spent time with her in the hospital, but only one friend visited. Once Paige went home on bed rest, the traffic picked up a little, but not much.

One friend came by with balloons and cookies from her favorite bakery. Her soccer team dropped by after a game. And a girl who had been Paige's biology partner brought dinner for the whole family, a generous act that touched Paige because it was so unexpected.

What Paige couldn't tell her visitors—because she might cry if she tried—was how grateful she was for their company. Having laughter to brighten her day and conversations to pass the time helped break up the monotony of a long recovery.

Surviving the car accident was an eye-opener for Paige. Of course life became more precious to her, but she also learned about the value of friends who show up.

After all, anyone can say they're thinking about you. Anyone can pray for a quick recovery. But those people who appear when you need them most—they are truly golden. Paige had a new respect and appreciation for friends like this. They had a special place in her heart because they had shown up.

.... ♥ ....

When Job's three friends . . . heard about all the troubles that had come upon him, they set out from their homes and met together by agreement to go and sympathize with him and comfort him.

—JOB 2:11

....

You Find Out Who Your Friends Are

You don't need me to tell you that our culture has watered down the definition of *friend*. It leads us to believe we have more real friends than we actually do based on our intangible digital connections.

But being in a group text with twenty other girls doesn't mean you have twenty trustworthy confidantes.

Having six hundred followers on Instagram doesn't mean you have six hundred faithful friends.

Numbers can be deceiving, and while social media certainly has an upside—it fosters community, offers a sense of belonging, and connects you with your peers—it can also create a false sense of security by making you think your friend base is larger than it is. It can blur the distinction between committed friends and casual friends.

Committed friends are those you carry through life. They have your back—and they will stand with you when others fall away.

Casual friends are those you have for a season of life or maybe a few seasons. You have fun together and your personalities click, but there isn't a great deal of loyalty or a deep heart connection.

Committed friends make up a small portion of your social network. Casual friends make up a large part.

Friendships can be tricky, and even the best friendships have ups and downs. But the real test of loyalty and commitment comes when your relationships get rocked. Like Paige in the opening story, you may find out who your true friends are when you face an unexpected rough patch.

The friends who surround you in a crisis, the friends who appear on your doorstep when you need them most, the friends who don't see you as a burden when you're hurting or struggling—these are all keepers.

These friends are worth your time and effort, and these relationships are most likely to go the distance as you enter adulthood.

I believe in treating everyone as friends until they give you a good reason not to. Keep the doors of your heart wide open because God will constantly bring new people into your life to shape you, challenge you, and walk with you.

At the same time, know who is in your corner. Invest in those friends who value you and make time for you, and make time for them too. You don't want to look back twenty years from now and realize that you poured yourself into all the wrong relationships. You don't want to miss out on the special moments that God has planned between you and a kindred soul.

The reality is, true and committed friends are rare. They can typically be counted on one hand—and if you have that, you're lucky.

Social media friends, on the other hand, are more like casual friends. They may sing your praises, they may seem loyal, but their commitment tends to be low. Depending on their mood and their opinion of your latest post, you may fall out of favor with them. Your relationships may last only a season or two, and when your life gets rocked, they may not come around.

···•··•••···•••···••···•••···•••···•• ♥ ···•••···••···•••···••···•••···•••···•··

Invest in those friends who value you and make time for you, and make time for them too.

···•··•••···•••···••···•••···••···•••···•••···••···•••···•••···•••···••···•··

Quick Quiz: How Loyal Are You?

Imagine that the leader of your friend group, Cassandra, has heard through the grapevine that another girl in your group, Lea, called Cassandra bossy and controlling. Lea said it to her boyfriend, and now Cassandra is livid.

Cassandra decides to teach Lea a lesson. Starting a new group text, she instructs everyone to ignore Lea. "Let's just not be friends with her," Cassandra writes, and immediately girls respond with either an "Okay" or a "Yes."

This plan doesn't sit well with you, probably because Cassandra *is* bossy and controlling and because you're tired of her manipulating the group. Somehow it has become everyone's job to keep Cassandra happy and fix things when she's mad or doesn't get her way.

The truth is, you truly like Lea. She's real, honest, and good-natured. You've sensed some tension lately between Cassandra and Lea and noticed Lea pulling away from the group. Although it may have been better for Lea to confront Cassandra directly, you don't blame her for wanting some space.

What do you do next?

A) You send a private text to Cassandra that reads, "Lea is my friend, and I'm not going to drop her over an incident between you two. Since this is personal, I think you and Lea should talk instead of getting the whole group involved."

B) You send Lea screenshots of the group texts with the comment, "Backstabber! Can you believe her?!" If Lea wants to start a war with Cassandra, you're in.

C) You reply "Okay" because you're scared to challenge Cassandra. Maybe one day you will, but for now you'll just be nice to Lea in secret so Cassandra doesn't find out.

D) You seriously rethink your friend group. Seeing everyone turn on Lea because Cassandra ordered it makes it painfully clear how easily they might turn on *you*. Who needs friends like that?

If you answered A or D, you're thinking correctly. True friends don't stir up drama, change their loyalty at another person's request, or let other people dictate who they can be friends with. Learn to think for yourself, trust your instincts, and ask God to let you know who to hang out with. Doing these things will not only make you a better friend, but they will also help you attract good people who know how to be friends and who will still be your friends down the road.

Does Social Media Have Power Over You?

If you monitor your social media numbers, as many girls do, you've probably seen how inconsistent people can be online. How many "likes" and comments your posts attract can vary significantly.

For instance, you might get a big response to a photo of you holding up a huge red snapper you caught at the beach. You may feel special, popular, and incredibly loved because your "likes" just hit a new record high.

But in your next post, the reverse can happen. You may get half as many "likes" on the photo of you surfing and hit a new record *low*.

This might make you wonder what you did wrong and why your peeps suddenly stopped liking you. Feeling defeated and embarrassed, you may delete the picture and pledge to never post anything related to surfing again because clearly that's not what people want.

Sound familiar? If so, then you probably give social media too much power in your life. You're using it to affirm your worth and gauge the quality of your friendships.

This is a mistake because you can have millions of "likes" but no genuine, committed friends. On the other hand, you can have three "likes" on a picture—and look very unpopular—yet have a best friend in real life who would walk through fire for you.

So I ask you, which would you prefer: ten thousand online friends or one real friend? People who show up regularly to "like" your pictures online or a person who shows up with your favorite latte in hand and stories to make you giggle when you don't make the volleyball team?

Technology doesn't offer proof that you have a thriving social life. *While technology can add value to your personal relationships, it isn't meant to replace them.*

The best connections happen in person. They involve making eye contact, hearing each other's voices, sharing laughter and tears, hugging, and experiencing the comfort, love, and affection that only a live human being can offer.

It's good to have online friendships, but I encourage you to keep them in perspective. Invest in them *after* you invest in real-life relationships because those matter most.

········· ♥ ·········

While technology can add value to your personal relationships, it isn't meant to replace them.

········· ♡ ·········

Five Truths About Friends

Here are five truths about real friendship and why it's best to use technology as a tool of friendship rather than an indicator of your social status.

1. God created you to connect with friends, not collect friends. It may be tempting to chase popularity online and get wrapped up in numbers that claim to tell you how you stack up against your peers.

But a booming social media fan club doesn't mean your relationships are booming too. You could have a wide reach across the globe—yet never deeply impact anyone.

Real relationships grow when you establish genuine connections. Even if you enjoy massive popularity online, it will never compare to the deeply satisfying joy of having even one or two real friends who know you completely and love you all the same.

2. Online friends and followers are fickle. They may "like" you one day and "unlike" you the next. They may "friend" you with joy and "unfriend" you in anger.

If you know this up front, you won't have unrealistic expectations of your online network. And you won't be devastated if their affection toward you changes because you know who your real friends are.

3. Too much time on technology breeds loneliness. We all escape into our phones when we're bored or lonely. But the irony is, this strategy can backfire. The very feelings we want to escape are often heightened because spending too much time online can have a counterintuitive effect.

It makes us *more* lonely.

Five months after my first book released, I woke up one day feeling really lonely. I realized that I was missing my friends! I had been so busy that most of my friend correspondence was occurring through text messages. My life had become a whirlwind of meeting deadlines, blogging, growing my online communities, and preparing for speaking events, and between those activities and caring for my family, I had little time for friendships.

This created a void in my life, and suddenly I realized how desperately that void needed attention. So I took time off from writing and speaking, and I started calling my friends instead of texting. I met people for lunch and coffee. I stopped turning down invitations and started engaging in real life again. Before long, I no longer felt that void. The joy of my friendships was filling it.

Technology can strengthen friendships, but it can also become a crutch if you let it. It can leave you feeling disconnected and alone. So set healthy boundaries for yourself, and limit your time online. Interact with friends in the real world, and when you do feel lonely, know that it's time to reach out in person.

4. Technology depersonalizes friendships. A while back, I spoke with a fifteen-year-old girl who received many text messages and Instagram posts on her birthday.

But only *one* friend called her.

The call came from an out-of-town friend, and it meant a lot because of the extra effort it required.

Technology is great for convenience, but it can make us lazy friends. We can take two seconds to "like" a friend's picture or ten seconds to text her a birthday message. Then we can check it off our mental list because our friend duty is complete.

A real friendship deserves more. A real friendship deserves at least a small effort like calling your friend on her birthday and singing "Happy Birthday" in that off-key voice of yours that she knows and loves.

Phone calls may seem old-fashioned, but people still appreciate getting them. A call adds the personal touch that often gets lost these days. Be the one person who calls your friend on her birthday, or better yet, show up at her house with a gift or surprise. Making a special effort for friends is always worth it, even if trends in technology suggest otherwise.

5. Real friends make everything better. Have you ever felt sad or upset, unable to stop dwelling on a problem, but once you talked to a friend, you immediately felt better?

Friends make pain bearable. A conversation that starts with you feeling overwhelmed and inconsolable may end with shared smiles and laughter. Even if your friend is short on solutions, she can offer what your discouraged heart needs most.

Hope.

None of us can handle life alone. None of us can thrive as islands. Your need for friends is God's way of drawing you closer to Him. Friends bring light into dark situations. Friends speak the truth and listen. Friends encourage you in uphill battles and faithfully cheer you on. Friends show you God's love in practical, everyday ways.

You'll meet a lot of friends in your life, and each one will serve a purpose. But the friendships worth holding sacred will have God's fingerprints all over them. These friends will show up just when you need them and with the perfect dose of wisdom.

Real friends are no accident. They are God's gift to you. He plants them in your life for a reason and as part of a greater plan.

······•··•••··•••••··••··•••••··••··••••·· ♥ ··•••••··••··•••••··••··•••••··••··

Two are better than one, because they have a good return for their labor: If either of them falls down, one can help the other up. But pity anyone who falls and has no one to help them up.

—ECCLESIASTES 4:9-10

······•··•••··•••••··••··•••••··••··•••••··••··•••••··••··•••••··••··•••••··••··

Know Who Has Your Back

Social media relationships can best be summarized in four words: "Easy come, easy go."

As I've said, the loyalty for online friends and relationships is typically low. There isn't much glue holding these relationships together.

Especially at your age—when most people use social media to project an image of their fabulous lives—being online is more likely to create feelings of jealousy, insecurity, and inadequacy than to meet your deepest friendship needs.

So enjoy your online friends, but know who has your back. Remember that the size of your social network does *not* reflect the quality of your friendships.

A small village of committed friends is far more valuable than a large community of casual friends. Friendships can certainly begin and be nurtured online, but your most life-changing moments will almost always occur in person.

Life will get harder as you grow up. You need friends who stand by you through thick and thin. And though it's great to have an online network, it's even better to have a real-life network.

After all, it's one thing to have friends you can count on for a daily "like"—and it's quite another to have friends you can count on to show up when you need them most.

··· •·······••··•·····••··•••···•• ❤ ···•·····•·····•··•••·····•··••·· ··

Friendships can certainly begin and be nurtured online, but your most life-changing moments will almost always occur in person.

··· •·······••··•·····••··•··•·····•··•·····••··•·····•··•·····•··••·· ··

❧ Discussion Questions ❧

1. Would you be willing to lose *all* your friends online to keep your *one* best friend in real life? Why or why not?

2. Imagine losing the Instagram account you spent three years building. On a scale of one to ten, how devastated would you be? What does your answer tell you about yourself?

3. Answer honestly: Are you a committed friend or a casual friend? After reading this chapter, are you inspired to be more committed to others? Why or why not?

4. Have you ever had online friends who adored you one day and ignored you the next? If so, how did it make you feel?

5. What's the most loyal thing a friend has done for you? What impact did it have on your sense of loyalty to her?

6. Sometimes in hard times casual friends show up like committed friends. Has this ever happened to you? If so, what did you learn?

Connection

 Relationships grow deeper
through face-to-face interaction.
Focus on depth and connections,
not numbers and screens.

Sometimes cell phones could be downright exhausting. At least that's how Alice felt.

Unlike most teenagers, she didn't care much about her phone. She didn't like being at parties and seeing everyone on their phones instead of talking.

Why shut people out in a social setting? she wondered. *Why waste the whole night doing the same thing you can do at home?*

At Alice's birthday party, one group of girls stayed only fifteen minutes—just long enough to get a photo. They wanted people to know they'd been invited to three events in one night, and they posted the pictures online to prove it. Once the girls accomplished their mission at Alice's party, they left. They hadn't even said "Hi," "Bye," or "Happy Birthday!" to Alice.

And the kicker? They captioned the picture they took at the

party *Girls' night!* The fact that these girls didn't even acknowledge Alice's birthday or her party felt like a second slap in the face.

Alice had always loved hanging out with her friends, but she missed the days when they could relax and have fun without making everything a photo shoot. Her friends were so obsessed with getting "likes" and comments that all their conversations revolved around finding the best angles, locations, and looks to achieve the best photos.

On weekends, the competition amped up. Alice noticed that many girls documented every place they went and tagged every person they'd been with to prove they had had the best night and more fun than anyone else.

It all made Alice ask herself, *What's the point? Were girls trying to make themselves look good—or make other girls feel bad? And when did friendships start needing evidence? Why did girls care so much about what people think of them and their social lives?*

Alice missed the days when she knew every detail about her friends. They'd stay up late talking about their latest crushes and what they'd said.

But now when her friends came over, they stayed glued to their phones. Instead of talking about their crushes, they Snapchatted with them, making Alice feel alone and left out of the conversation.

The weird thing was, nobody else seemed bothered by this. Nobody else seemed sad that cell phones were putting a wedge in their friendships.

More than anything, Alice longed for her friends' undivided attention again. She wanted to have uninterrupted conversations in which her thoughts and opinions mattered.

Lately, it hadn't been that way at all. Alice felt like she was always competing with cell phones and coming in second place every single time.

······•••·····•••·····•••·····•••···· ♥ ···•••·····•••·····•••·····•••·····•••···

> "Do to others as you would
> like them to do to you."
> **—LUKE 6:31** NLT

···•••·····•••·····•••·····•••·····•••·····•••···•••·····•••·····•••·····•••···

The Gift of Your Presence

Have you ever been out with your friends and suddenly looked around to notice that everyone is on their phones?

If you haven't experienced this yet, you will. And chances are, your automatic instinct will be to escape into your phone as well because what else can you do with nobody to talk to?

Digital devices have become a normal and familiar part of your social scene. As you grow accustomed to seeing them, it may no longer bother you when friends choose technology over your company.

But at some point, it probably has bothered you. You may have related to Alice's sentiments in the opening story, feeling that small pang of rejection as you realized that you apparently weren't entertaining enough to keep a friend's attention. He or she would rather cruise the Internet or Snapchat with someone else than personally engage with you.

As I've said, technology is a great tool, but too often these days it is used to *replace* face-to-face interactions rather than *enhance* them. What should be a bonus—a great tool to help you stay connected—has instead become the primary means of connecting.

As a result, people feel lonely, isolated, and disengaged. Instead of looking at faces, we stare at screens. We've created a social phenomenon where we're hanging out with friends, yet we escape into private worlds.

It's almost comical how compulsively we check our online newsfeeds so we don't miss out on anything, but the real joke is on us because ignoring the people around us causes us to miss out on the best social encounters of all—those face-to-face, eye-to-eye, heart-to-heart, give-each-other-a-hug encounters. Technology can create relationship gaps, like the one Alice sensed with her friends, that only grow wider with time.

How many important interactions have you let pass by because you were engrossed in your digital device?

What conversations have you failed to have that might have provided you—or someone else—with *exactly* what was needed on a hard day?

The best connection you can make is with the person in front of you. The best gift you can offer friends is the gift of your presence.

So use your phone to plan a movie night—and then put your phone away when you're at the movie and getting coffee afterward. Choose the camaraderie of your friends over the crutch of your phone. Be fully present with the people you're with.

Make your face-to-face time together count. Give your friends your undivided attention. Focus on the people in front of you, and you'll see your friendships deepen.

··· •······••··••··••··••··••··••··· ❤ ···•··••··•···••··••··••··••··· ··

Make your face-to-face time together count.
Give your friends your undivided attention.
Focus on the people in front of you.

··· •······••··••··•··••··••···••··••··••··••··••··••··••··••··••··••··•· ··

Settling a Restless Heart

It's hard to break an addiction, and a technology addiction is no exception.

Before a person can break an addiction, however, he or she must first admit to having one.

Technology addictions have become so common that they're easily justifiable. You can compare yourself to people you think *really* have a problem—like the girl who carries her phone around as if it's life support—and convince yourself that you're actually doing fine.

But the truth is, we all have room to improve. We'd all be wise to consider the balance we strike between the real world and the virtual world so our relationships don't suffer.

I believe the root cause of technology addiction is restlessness. We have a restlessness in our hearts that we can't shake off or ignore for very long. We have a desperate need to feel loved, at peace, secure, and purposeful—and technology offers an easy and instant fix.

But that fix wears off quickly. The temporary high ends. And before long, we need another fix to settle our anxious hearts. We pick up our phones to get it since phones are easy and convenient.

That restlessness, however, can never be settled by technology because it's meant to be settled by God. Only God can lead you and me to a place of deep, genuine calm.

As Saint Augustine said, "You have made us for yourself, O Lord, and our heart is restless until it rests in you."[5]

This world will demand your constant time and attention. It will distract you with dings, beeps, and digital notifications. If you let it, it will suck you into the black hole of the Internet, and it will lead you to mistakenly believe that life's most pressing questions can be answered with a Google search rather than a God search.

This is why it's up to you to set wise and healthy limits to your use of technology. You might even ask your parents or an adult you trust to help you keep those limits so you have time for God and the good life He has planned for you.

That good life includes friendship. It involves strong female connections that He will use to help you become the young woman He created you to be. If you haven't found good friends yet, please don't worry. God's got it under control, and He will guide you to friends who will enrich your life.

In the meantime, practice being a good friend. Work on getting your head and heart in the right place. While there is no formula for being a good friend, there are certain principles that can help you.

> May the words of my mouth and the meditation of my heart be pleasing to you, O LORD, my rock and my redeemer.
> —PSALM 19:14 NLT

Ten Ways to Deepen Your Friendships

By practicing the ten habits outlined here, you can build meaningful connections that offer more than a short-lived fix for your restlessness or a temporary break from your aloneness.

1. Be real. This guideline is common sense, yet living it out is difficult to do. After all, when you live in a world that expects girls to be perfect, who wants to admit they're falling short of that ideal?

Social media promotes the appearance of perfection. It allows you to create a digital identity and build an image that draws comments like "You're so perfect! I want to be you!" and "Goals!" and "Can I have your life?"

Comments like these are very common among teen girls, and while they're great for your ego, they aren't so great for your relationships.

That's because constructing a perfect image hides the real you, and that real you is the girl who people can relate to best. That ideal image also makes you afraid of ever looking less than perfect.

But the reality is, nobody's life is a constant dream. Nobody is even close to perfect. This is why we need Jesus—because He *is* perfect, and His power is made perfect in our weakness (2 Corinthians 12:9).

The real you attracts real friends, so be honest about yourself in person and online. Remember that the people worth having in your life don't need a filter to see the best in you.

2. Control your jealousy. Nothing ruins a relationship faster than envy. Once again, I wish I could tell you that you'll totally outgrow this ugly monster, but that isn't true.

You'll never be completely free from this emotion. You can, however, learn to successfully control your jealousy so it doesn't control you.

The first step is to be honest. Admit to yourself, *Okay, I'm jealous of my friend. I'm having bad thoughts about her that aren't right. I want to love my friend and be happy for her without feeling sorry for myself.*

Once you acknowledge this, you can pray. Ask God to help you see your friend as *He sees her* and love her as *He loves her.*

The easing of your envy probably won't happen immediately. But if you consistently and genuinely pray this prayer, your heart will change. You'll find yourself less inclined to dwell on negative or bitter thoughts.

Proverbs 4:23 says, "Above all else, guard your heart, for everything you do flows from it." By making deliberate efforts to lock jealousy out of your heart—and by recognizing when envy does seep in—you can truly love your friends and genuinely celebrate their blessings without harboring any secret resentments.

3. Avoid the comparison trap. Like jealousy, comparison separates you from your friends. You'll either feel superior or inferior, prideful or insecure, and not one of these scenarios is helpful.

God created all of us with various abilities. He has equipped you and your friends with different gifts given by the same Holy Spirit (1 Corinthians 12:4). So instead of comparing yourselves to one another, unite. Each of you can be stronger together than you can be alone.

If you're trying out for cheerleading, for instance, and you notice other girls struggling to learn a routine you picked up easily, help them. Humble yourself by passing on what you know instead of feeling better by comparison. Someday you may be the one needing help.

When that day does come and you're bummed because your friend's talent outshines yours, do the opposite of what you feel like doing—and *compliment her.* Ask if she has any tips to help you. Be vulnerable. Let your need motivate you to stretch beyond your comfort zone by revealing your need. This can help both your cheerleading and your friendships reach a new level of excellence.

Relationships grow when you choose to appreciate your friends' gifts while sharing your own. The more you root for others, the more they'll root for you and the less anyone will feel the need to compare and despair or compare and gloat.

4. Value kindness over popularity. The best friends are often hidden gems. They don't flaunt their awesomeness, seek attention, or try to impress the "in" crowd.

Many girls want popular friends, but it's better to have kind and genuine friends. Kind friends will go the distance: they grow up and become kind adults you can respect and admire. Kind friends have generous, thoughtful, compassionate spirits that friendships need in order to last.

Can kind girls be popular? Of course. But making popularity the starting point for choosing friends isn't wise. In today's world, having good morals doesn't typically help teen girls gain social status. Virtues like kindness are best appreciated with time and maturity. Sometimes people need to experience what selfish friends are like before they can truly value genuine kindness.

First Corinthians 13:4 says, "Love is patient, love is kind. It does not envy, it does not boast, it is not proud." Where love exists, so will kindness. So choose friends who live out these aspects of love. Recognize the value of people who make you feel good, and make them feel good as well.

5. Forgive easily and often. Only God can love perfectly. The rest of us do the best we can. So while it's important to choose friends who treat you well, keep your expectations realistic.

We all fall short of the glory of God, and in any relationship that lasts for a significant length of time, you're bound to encounter conflict.

Be prepared for this. Make it a habit to forgive your friends easily and often, remembering that as you forgive others, God forgives you (Matthew 6:14).

Let me clarify, however, that I'm *not at all* suggesting you become a doormat and keep your grievances bottled up. This just turns you into a volcano ready to explode. What I am suggesting is keeping an open dialogue with your friends so that little grudges don't turn into big issues. Be honest with your friend when she hurts your feelings—and humbly listen when she tells you how you've hurt her. By practicing forgiveness on a small level every day (like letting it go when your friend invites someone else to the beach), you'll grow more capable of handling any bigger injustices that come.

Many friends are quick to anger, but few are quick to forgive. While some betrayals may mean you need time to heal—giving you a good reason to distance yourself—you can work toward loving everyone with a resentment-free heart. But love wisely.

This means loving your best friends up close and personal, and loving the people you don't trust from a distance. Don't share your deepest secrets with them, but don't pretend they don't exist either.

Jesus' example of forgiveness offers many powerful lessons. He knew from the beginning which disciple would betray Him (John 6:64), yet He kept Judas in His inner circle. Jesus didn't withhold His love. Later, even as Jesus suffered on the cross, He asked God to forgive those who tortured Him, saying, "Father, forgive them, for they do not know what they are doing" (Luke 23:34).

This kind of forgiveness is unfathomable to most of us, yet it's the standard God has set. God calls you to love and forgive generously, drawing on strength from Jesus when the hurt seems unbearable.

6. Build bridges, not walls. Friendships can't grow when people feel the need to guard and protect themselves. Keeping your guard up builds walls; letting your guard down builds bridges.

Friends drop their guard when they feel safe in your company. How do you foster a feeling of safety with other girls? Here are a few ways:

♡ Drop your guard by being real and honest.
♡ Seek to understand your friends' points of view.
♡ Treat girls as allies, not competitors.

♡ Avoid jumping to conclusions or assuming the worst about
people.

♡ Create a comfortable environment (e.g. pajamas and no
makeup) for deep discussions.

♡ Hold your tongue when critical thoughts come to mind.

♡ Show your friends the grace and love God shows you.

Jesus was a bridge builder, and when you "take captive every
thought to make it obedient to Christ" (2 Corinthians 10:5), you
become a bridge builder too. As you learn to center your thought
life on Him, He enables you to create an atmosphere of love and
trust.

7. Respect that your friends will have other friends.

When you meet a girl you really click with, it may be hard to give
her space. You may feel possessive and not want to share your friend
for fear of losing her.

This fear is understandable—but it's unfair to your friend.
When you truly love your friend, you want to introduce her to
everyone you know so they can see how awesome she is too.

Could sharing your friend lead her to a new BFF? Possibly, but
that risk exists even if you kept your friend all to yourself because
nobody likes to feel smothered or controlled.

We all want the freedom to choose other friends. To claim
exclusive rights to a person will only push her away.

So love your friends well, but give them space to explore other
friendships. Explore other friendships for yourself too. And regardless of how many friends you have, you can choose to be content.
Remember Paul's words in Philippians 4:11–13:

I am not saying this because I am in need, for I have learned to
be content whatever the circumstances. I know what it is to be

in need, and I know what it is to have plenty. I have learned the secret of being content in any and every situation, whether well fed or hungry, whether living in plenty or in want. I can do all this through him who gives me strength.

Friendship shouldn't be stressful. So keep your friendships healthy by not suffocating or putting too much pressure on any one person.

8. Treat your friends like a close-knit family. If you look at any strong family, you'll notice a few common threads:

- ♡ Devotion
- ♡ Protectiveness
- ♡ A refusal to give up on one another

In fact, it's usually a crisis or emergency that brings out the best in a strong family. Despite the tension that adversity can create, it can also tighten the unit. It brings the troops together. It makes everyone rally around the family member who needs help.

All of us want friendships that offer similar security. We want friends who aren't scared off when our circumstances get hard.

Embrace your friends like family. Love other girls like sisters because they are your sisters in Christ. And when adversity strikes, unite. Don't let your sister walk alone.

When you go through tough times, you'll want your friends to be there for you. So when your friends are in their darkest hours, be there for them.

9. Do random acts of love. It doesn't take much to make a friend smile—or to make her day. Taking even a few minutes to show you care helps deepen a friendship.

You make a friend feel special when you:

♡ Bake a cake for her birthday.
♡ Plan a surprise party to celebrate her recent achievement.
♡ Create a funny video or picture collage of your favorite memories.
♡ Compile a playlist of her favorite songs.
♡ Tie helium balloons to her mailbox when she makes a team.
♡ Decorate her locker "just because."

There are a thousand ways to show love to your friend, so be creative. Consider what speaks to her heart. What excites her and makes her laugh? Your thoughtful action will be appreciated now and may be a fond memory in the future.

In John 13:35, Jesus said, "By this everyone will know that you are my disciples, if you love one another." With your special and unexpected acts of love, you show your friends you care.

10. Put God at the heart of your relationships. When God's Spirit lives in a person, it shows. The fruit of the Holy Spirit—those nine virtues of a godly life—become evident.

Following are the nine fruits named in Galatians 5:22–23 (NLT):

♡ Love
♡ Joy
♡ Peace
♡ Patience
♡ Kindness
♡ Goodness
♡ Faithfulness
♡ Gentleness
♡ Self-control

First John 4:7–8 says, "Dear friends, let us love one another, for love comes from God. Everyone who loves has been born of God and knows God. Whoever does not love does not know God, because God is love."

God gives you the ability to love. He reveals Himself to you when others love you. By centering your relationships on God, you gain an anchor. You can enjoy a spiritual connection that makes every connection deeper and richer.

Talk to your friends about God, share Scripture with them, and don't hesitate to dive into conversations about your faith. Look beyond physical appearances as you seek to connect spiritually. Let your friends' love teach you about Christ's love even as you show Christlike love to them.

Above all, remember to pass on the love you receive. This is how friendships grow—and how God's kingdom advances.

❤

When you go through tough times, you'll want your friends to be there for you. So when your friends are in their darkest hours, be there for them.

Look Up from Your Phone

It's interesting to think that God holds the universe He created in the palm of His hand—and meanwhile here we are, palming our cell phones.

As God smiles at us, His favorite creation, we're often staring at our screens. With our eyes cast down, we miss the splendor of the world He made for us to enjoy, a world of sunsets, blue skies, and fascinating people.

I imagine God saying, "Take a break. Look up. Enjoy this vibrant life all around you. It's My gift to you!"

Don't miss God's gifts because of the technology you hold in your hand. That technology is good and beneficial *when it's used properly*. I believe God gave the masterminds behind technological advances their talents to enrich the lives of others, and there's a purpose they're meant to serve.

But no matter how advanced technology gets or how many cool apps and gadgets are introduced, their value will never come close to matching the value of connecting in person.

God created you and me to need face-to-face interaction. And when you do spend time with people in person, something extraordinary happens: your relationships gain depth, strength, and significance.

The best moments of life are waiting for you, but you'll need to look up from your phone and take notice. All you have to do is engage with the world instead of escaping into your phone. Enjoy the people in front of you while you have the opportunity.

We are merely moving shadows, and all
our busy rushing ends in nothing.

—PSALM 39:6 NLT

❧ Discussion Questions ☙

1. How do you feel when a friend seems more interested in technology than in being with you?

2. Do you or your parents limit your daily screen time? Why or why not? What kinds of boundaries and self-discipline can enable healthy technology habits?

3. In what ways, if any, do your technology habits hurt your real-life friendships? What will you do to break those technology habits?

4. When you're lonely or restless, are you more likely to reach for your phone or reach out to a person? Why? Is praying an option you consider? Why or why not?

5. What was the deepest conversation you've ever had with a friend? How did you know you could safely share with her?

6. Would you rather be "liked" online or loved in person? What's the difference between the two?

Wisdom

 Being left out or excluded can make you feel rejected and forgotten. Learning to deal wisely with your emotions protects your relationships and self-worth.

*L*acey was perfectly content to stay home on Friday night, watch a movie with her family, and eat pizza in her pajamas.

But then she made the mistake of checking Instagram. As she scrolled through pictures, she realized she hadn't been invited to a party. Immediately her mood tanked because everyone she knew was dressed up and having a blast.

"Unforgettable night!" one girl posted.

"Best band ever!" wrote another girl, posing with the lead singer.

"Squad goals!" said a third post, a group selfie that included two of Lacey's closest friends.

Lacey's newsfeed was blowing up with posts from this party, so she was able to piece together the puzzle. Apparently a girl in Lacey's PE class was hosting a birthday bash complete with a

Motown band, a photo booth, and a lavish theme. The girls were dressed in sequins, and the guys wore coats and ties.

Everyone looked dazzling—and utterly glamorous.

Lacey glanced down at her fleece pajamas and the pizza stain on her shirt. Between that and the family-friendly flick she was watching with her little brother, she suddenly felt like a loser.

Each Instagram picture felt like a dagger in Lacey's heart. Despite the pain, she couldn't stop looking. She kept scrolling and scrolling, constantly refreshing her newsfeed to see the latest posts.

The irony was, Lacey felt more betrayed by her friends than the host. Why hadn't her friends mentioned the party? Why did she find out about it on Instagram? Had her friends talked about it behind her back, conspiring to keep it a secret? Or was this an intentional effort to paint Lacey as a social outcast by posting all their pictures at once so her absence could be noted?

A tornado of anger began stirring in Lacey's chest—and she wanted the tornado out before it ripped her apart inside.

Lacey decided to vent on social media. She wanted her friends to know she was hurt. One by one, she commented on their pictures, hoping to make them feel guilty.

Looks like a great party, Eliza . . . except that I'm not there!

Wow, guys, best friends forever.

#traitors #hangingoutwithoutme #forgetit

Posting these comments made Lacey feel a little better, but it didn't change the situation. She was still stuck at home feeling like a dork. She still had a tornado in her chest. She still had pictures in her newsfeed that highlighted her alienation.

Why were relationships so difficult? How was Lacey supposed to like herself, as the adults in her life always emphasized, when her best friends didn't seem to like her or want her around?

Deep down, Lacey wondered if she deserved to be left out.

Maybe her friends had simply discovered what she'd known all along—that she really was a loser, and as hard as she had tried to conceal that, her cover had finally been blown.

·····•····•••····••···••····••···••····• ♥ ·····••····•••····••···••···••····••···

Fools vent their anger, but the wise quietly hold it back.
—PROVERBS 29:11 NLT

·····•····•••····•••····•···••····••····•••···••····••···••····•••···••····••···

Rejection Hurts

One of the best feelings in the world is to be *wanted*.

And one of the worst feelings in the world is to be *rejected*.

We've all experienced rejection, right? Rejection takes many forms and provokes that terrible feeling of not being good enough to make the cut, whether for a party, a friend group, an athletic team, a love interest, or something else you really care about.

In times of rejection, the actual event may not hurt you the most, but rather the emotions that get triggered as the hurt settles in your heart. These emotions may include:

- Self-doubt
- Insecurity
- Loneliness
- Confusion
- Stress
- Anxiety
- Anger
- Resentment
- Fear of insignificance

As emotions like these get tangled, it's difficult to think clearly or act reasonably. It's hard to see or believe the supreme truths about you, God's love, your situation, and the people involved.

Like Lacey's frame of mind in the opening story, your judgment can become clouded. As you feel the sharp sting of rejection, you may act impulsively and foolishly. These actions may provide short-term relief, but they will create long-term problems that ultimately hurt your relationships and your sense of self-worth.

Why does rejection hurt so much? I think the reason is fear. All of us want to be liked, loved, and desired, but we fear that we're unlikable, unlovable, and undesirable.

We work hard to prove that we're a *Somebody* because deep down we fear we're a *Nobody*—and if anyone discovers this, they won't give us the time of day.

Accepting this mindset sets you up to lose. It prompts you to build a case against yourself. Consciously or not, you start to catalog every rejection you receive as evidence that your secret worries are correct:

- *Of course they rejected me—I'm a joke.*
- *Nobody likes me. My life has no meaning or purpose.*
- *I'm just another warm body taking up space on earth.*

These things are *not true*, of course, but it's hard to convince yourself of that when you're reeling from rejection and feeling vulnerable.

Fortunately, God can help. God can salvage hard situations and remind you to trust your faith above your feelings. After all, feelings are fickle. They're up, they're down, they're all over the place—and they change for good reasons, for random reasons, and for no reason at all.

Just because you *feel* like a disappointment doesn't mean you *are* a disappointment.

Just because you *feel* worthless doesn't mean you *are* worthless.

Remember that your feelings are important, but they can mislead you. They can prompt you to make decisions based on emotion rather than wisdom. And since God is the source of all wisdom, it's important to go to Him first, especially when your heart is unsettled and your head is in a fog.

I know it's tempting to take every wound and grievance you have straight to social media, but it's better to take them straight to God. Let Him be the first voice that speaks to your broken heart. Let Him hear your prayers and replace your faulty thoughts with His truths, reminding you that even when you're overlooked, your life matters to Him in a big way.

········· ♥ ·········

Just because you *feel* like a disappointment
doesn't mean you *are* a disappointment.
Just because you *feel* worthless
doesn't mean you *are* worthless.

·········

How Will You Handle Your Pain?

Whenever your feelings get hurt, it's helpful to stop and ask yourself this question: *How will I handle this?*

The easiest solution is to let your emotions be the boss of you and go with your knee-jerk reaction.

If you're mad, you yell.

If you're frustrated, you vent.

If you're sad or crushed, you withdraw, hole up, and refuse to face the world.

Letting your emotions control you, however, can cause tremendous damage. Left to their own devices, emotions can knock things around without any regard to consequences and blaze a path of destruction through your life and other people's lives as well. The end result is a mess of broken pieces and shattered parts for you to clean up.

Letting your emotions loose on people can damage your relationships, but internalizing them and burying them down deep can damage you. Neither option is healthy. In both cases, the problem grows.

The wiser solution is to ask God to help you control your emotions. Rather than act on your feelings, identify them and then work through them. Practice self-control and wait until you're in a more rational state of mind before responding to a situation.

Sound impossible? It's not. With the help of the Holy Spirit, you can resist knee-jerk reactions. You can fix your mind on God's truths and open your heart to His will so that, even if you feel the need to address a hurtful incident, you can act with dignity, grace, and self-control.

♥

No discipline is enjoyable while it is happening—it's painful! But afterward there will be a peaceful harvest of right living for those who are trained in this way.

—HEBREWS 12:11 NLT

>>> ... ♡ ... <<<

Eight Ways to Deal with Hard Emotions

Here are eight tips to help you manage hard emotions that come with social letdowns as well as experiences that trigger your insecurities. It's good to learn early how to handle those difficult feelings that can turn you into someone you're not.

1. Pray for God to calm your heart and mind. The first step to take when your emotions flare up is to find a quiet place to talk to God. Pour out your heart and tell Him exactly how you feel.

Nothing you say can surprise God because He already knows you completely. He invites you to share every pain in your heart, and He is patient as you wrestle through complex issues. When you go to Him when you're upset, you show your trust in Him.

That growing trust is God's work inside you, and that growth matters more than any event that happens to you. When you turn to the Lord with your hurt and anger, He provides strength, comfort, wisdom, and direction. Like the disciples in Acts 4:13, you can become bold and courageous by spending time with Jesus.

God can soothe a racing mind and a restless heart. He can clear distractions from your head and reveal a wise course of action. Even in uncertainty, He can give you peace. He's your ultimate security, the anchor you can count on for anything anytime.

2. Recognize your fears. What keeps you up at night? What do you worry about most? What fears and insecurities surface when your social life gets rocked?

Fear seems so personal, yet it's actually universal. We all have fears that get the best of us and make us panic or overreact.

Normal fears include:

- Fear that nobody likes you.
- Fear that nobody wants you.
- Fear that you're not funny, cool, smart, or pretty enough.
- Fear of missing out.
- Fear of getting left behind.
- Fear of not fitting in.
- Fear of being ridiculed.
- Fear of losing friends.
- Fear of having a lousy social life.
- Fear of being alone.
- Fear of being forgotten.
- Fear that you don't deserve love.
- Fear that your inner critic is right and you are unlovable.

Identifying your fears can help you better understand and deal with hard emotions.

- *Why am I jealous that my best friend found a new friend? Because I fear I'm being replaced.*
- *Why am I distraught that they didn't tag me in that picture? Because I fear I'm being pushed out of the circle.*
- *Why am I freaking out that I don't have a homecoming date? Because I fear that I am unlikable and will never find a boy who likes me.*

Fear isn't from God; it's from Satan, a dark power whose mission is to separate you from God. Satan wants you to live in fear because it breaks your trust in God. The fact that the most repeated phrase in the Bible is "Do not fear" makes it pretty clear what God thinks of fear. He knows how it imprisons you and distances you from Him.

Satan is no match for God, for the One who lives in you is greater than the one who lives in the world (1 John 4:4). The best way to get a handle on your fears is to name them, face them, and conquer them by repeating God's truth and letting it fill you with comfort and confidence.

3. Give it a day. Acting when your emotions run high often leads to words and actions you'll regret. Even if you're level-headed by nature, it takes time for your emotions to settle.

Unless the situation is an emergency of some kind—which it rarely is—give yourself time to cool down before you respond to a hurtful event. Maybe you'll need a day. At least take a few hours. Talk to God first, and if you're still short on answers, seek the counsel of your parents, a wise friend, or a mentor.

If the hurt is big enough to create a rift between you and a friend, think about the best approach that will still enable a long-term relationship. Choose your words carefully so she'll listen and not automatically get defensive.

Psalm 141:3 (NLT) says, "Take control of what I say, O LORD, and guard my lips." Turn to God for direction. He can give you the words to say and the most effective way to say them.

4. Be empowered. You were made to be proactive, not reactive. God wants you to take control of your life, not live at the mercy of external events beyond your control.

You do yourself a disservice if you think like this: *I'm never invited to parties. Teachers never call on me. Boys never look at me. Teams never want me.* The problem with this mindset is that it keeps you waiting.

Waiting to be invited.

Waiting to be noticed.

Waiting to be chosen.

But guess what? You don't have to wait! You don't have to sit around hoping and waiting for something spectacular to happen.

A great life isn't something you're given, but rather something you create by pouring yourself into people and personal passions.

When you get rejected, you have a choice to make: you can dwell on what happened, or you can take action to lift your spirits. The first is a passive response; the second, an empowered choice.

Is it okay to cry all weekend because you were cut out of plans? Sure. But the empowered choice is to make other plans.

Is it understandable that you might stay glued to Instagram like Lacey did even though it mangles your heart? Yes. But the empowered response is to put away your phone, return to your family, and enjoy the rest of the movie night at home.

Second Timothy 1:7 says, "The Spirit God gave us does not make us timid, but gives us power, love and self-discipline."

Remembering that you have a degree of control over your life will help you deal with rejection. It allows you to bounce back and move on instead of waiting for something that may never come.

5. Know your worth. Being rejected can feel like being put on the clearance table. Comparing yourself to the girls in high demand, you may falsely assume that your life is worthless.

But what matters most to God can't be measured. Even when you feel unwanted or overlooked, you are infinitely valuable to Him.

The world will tell you that your worth is determined using a moving scale. It will calculate your worth based on changing statistics such as:

♡ How many friends you have.

♡ How many followers you attract.

♡ How many "likes" your pictures get.

♡ How many invitations you receive each weekend.

But the truth, my friend, is that these numbers fade away. They don't last. Besides, God makes everything—including your life—beautiful in its time (Ecclesiastes 3:11), and in your peak seasons and your slumps, He keeps His hand on you.

6. Know who's good for you. Some people aren't good for you. They cause more stress, tears, and drama than genuine joy, laughter, and happiness.

Be kind to everyone, but distance yourself from negativity. Trust your gut instincts when you feel like a friend or a group you spend time with would drop you in a heartbeat or purposely leave you out. These instincts are usually correct.

Friends who treat you inconsistently can be called 50/50 friends. They may love you one day, but they'll ignore you the next. You're never sure where you stand, and their loyalty to you is low.

Real friends, on the other hand, are *consistent*. They respect you, and they are there for you from day to day. When they hurt your feelings, it's not intentional. They own up to their mistakes, value your friendship, and love you despite your flaws.

Relationships with real friends give you the courage to be yourself. Toxic relationships crush your spirit. Learning to recognize when a relationship isn't working, and being brave enough to walk away when you see warning signs that it might be toxic, is an important life skill to develop.

Proverbs 13:20 (NLT) says, "Walk with the wise and become wise; associate with fools and get in trouble." When you choose your circle of friends wisely, you will surround yourself with the kind of love and support that builds confidence, self-worth, and a sense of belonging.

7. Turn your pain into a purpose. One wise way to cope with rejection is to convert it into good. Since God is the God of all comfort, He wants you to take the comfort He gives you in tough times and later use it to comfort others (2 Corinthians 1:3–7). That is how good comes out of rejection.

Rejection loses its power when you repurpose it. When you let an incident of hurt make you more loving, you redefine that incident. You start a new series of actions that point to and please God.

Also, realize that there is power in pain. If you study the life of any world changers, you'll often find that their passion has its roots in some pain from their past. The founder of an anti-bullying organization, for instance, may be a woman who was bullied as a child. An advocate for fatherless children may be a man whose father deserted him.

Letting rejection motivate you to do good keeps it from destroying you. So lean into your hurt and discomfort. Ask God what you can learn from it. Pain can be a great teacher, and when you learn lessons from your pain, you help yourself and can then go on to help others.

8. Recognize the real ache. The deep ache inside you that often masquerades as a desire for more friends, more attention, more invitations, or more acceptance is really an ache for God.

God created you for your final home in heaven. He designed you to need Him and long for Him. Inside you is a God-sized hole, and while stuffing friends, parties, and other earthly blessings into that hole may work temporarily, eventually the hole will open back up unless you're letting Him fill it.

Some of your heart's desires can't be met on this side of heaven.

And as Sissy Goff of Daystar Counseling Ministries in Nashville tells her teen clients, it's important to know what to do with those longings you have that can only be satisfied for short spurts.

You'll never achieve perfect peace and happiness on earth. You'll never find the *perfect* group of friends, the *perfect* boyfriend, or the *perfect* circumstances.

So when your life fails to shape up the way you planned or expected, don't assume it's all wrong. Don't convince yourself that your future is hopeless simply because your life looks different than you once imagined it looking at this point.

God has a plan for you, and whatever disappointment or adversity you face, you can recover. You can bounce back with more resilience and strength. That's a promise Jesus made: "In this world you will have trouble. But take heart! I have overcome the world" (John 16:33).

So, yes, you'll get hurt in this life, but realize that the real ache inside you runs deeper than the ache that comes with relationship stress. When you feel it, turn to Christ. Let Him give you the peace you're yearning for and the wisdom to remember what your real goal is.

The deep ache inside you that often masquerades as a desire for more friends, more attention, more invitations, or more acceptance is really an ache for God.

The Ultimate Invitation

Let's face it: all of us get blinded by our emotions sometimes, especially after experiencing rejection.

We all have a nagging voice in our heads that tells us that more invitations + more friends + more acceptance = more security.

But the truth is, genuine security is found internally, not externally. It comes from having the ultimate *spiritual* experience, not the ultimate *social* experience.

Is it nice to be invited to parties? Is it reassuring when friend groups want you? Are your teen years more enjoyable when you're respected and viewed favorably by your peers?

Yes, absolutely. Without question, these things matter. But more important than how anyone else perceives you and receives you is how you perceive yourself.

After all, you're the one who must be kind to yourself even when life and people disappoint you.

Remember, the One who knows you best also loves you best. He isn't appalled by your flaws, He isn't put off by the times you experience rejection, and He won't abandon you when others kick you to the curb. Instead He draws close to the brokenhearted (Psalm 34:18).

Your time of need is actually God's opportunity to do His best work because His power is made perfect in human weakness (2 Corinthians 12:9). When you need strength, God will empower you.

So rather than fear rejection, prepare for it. Prepare your heart in advance for those days when nobody seems to understand you, see you, or want you. God will give you the tools to deal wisely with these days. He can help you stay calm and think clearly rather than act on blind emotion.

The only invitation truly relevant to your destiny is your invitation to live with Christ. Everything else is a bonus. So concentrate on what's relevant. Keep the ultimate invitation locked away in your heart, and remember that as long as you have it, you have all the security you need.

Liked

· · • ··· • • • ·· • • • ··· • • ·· • • • ··· • • ·· • • ··· ♥ ··· • • • ·· • ··· • • • • ·· • • ··· • • • • ·· • • • ··· • • ··

"I am the Alpha and the Omega, the First
and the Last, the Beginning and the End."

—REVELATION 22:13

· · • ··· • • • ·· • • • ··· • • ·· • • • ··· • • ·· • • • ··· • • • ··· • • • • ·· • • ··· • • • • ·· • • ··· • • ··

❧ Discussion Questions ❧

1. On a scale of one to ten, how well do you bounce back after rejection? Why do you think it's easy or difficult for you?

2. When your feelings get hurt, do you usually act impulsively, or do you take time to cool off?

3. What are your three biggest relationship fears? Have you ever admitted these to anyone? Why or why not?

4. When, if ever, have you left out, excluded, or forgotten to include a friend? How did you feel afterward?

5. Who in your life handles their emotions wisely? What have you learned by watching that person handle hurt and disappointment?

6. When in your life has a rejection or another kind of disappointment that you experienced led to something good? (Example: Being left out of a party prompted you to reach out to a new friend who is now one of your closest friends.)

8

Humility

 God is calling you to a life of service and active faith, not fame and self-promotion.

By all appearances, Samantha was a good Christian girl. The daughter of a youth pastor, she'd spent her whole life telling people about Jesus.

Samantha knew a hundred Bible verses by heart. She wore a cross necklace every day. She posted Scripture on Instagram and videos on YouTube that taught people about God and salvation.

Church leaders celebrated Samantha as a role model for younger girls. Staying mindful of how these girls looked up to her kept Samantha on the right path. She prided herself on avoiding the mistakes that so many of her peers made.

Samantha knew God had big things in store for her. She felt certain that her hard work and efforts to stay pure would pay off tremendously.

So when people called her a Jesus freak or head of the God Squad, she focused on the big picture. She imagined herself as the most famous Christian on earth, speaking to worldwide audiences through television, radio, and sold-out events.

Already Samantha had gained notoriety with her online videos. Born with the gift of gab, she could win over an audience with ease and had attracted more than seven thousand YouTube subscribers in less than two months.

If Samantha kept growing at this rate, she'd be a viral sensation in no time. Her goal was to attain a million views in a year and grow a large fan base that would allow her to pursue other interests too, such as acting.

Samantha knew that breaking into Hollywood was unbelievably competitive. But as a famous Christian, she might have an advantage. Of course, her being vocal about God might not go over well in Hollywood, but Samantha would deal with that when and if she had to. For now she'd stay on this path because clearly she had found a niche.

Samantha dreamed of having keynote talks at major conferences, bestselling books, billboards, videos, and her own reality show, and she expected God to make all her dreams come true. Whenever a new opportunity arose, Samantha felt compelled to work even harder. The sky was the limit in what God could do for her and how famous she might ultimately become.

❤

> "These people honor me with their lips,
> but their hearts are far from me."
>
> **—MATTHEW 15:8**

Do You Love God—or Do You Use God?

It's probably fair to say that, at some point, most girls would like to be famous. They may not even care *what* they're famous for as long as it's something good.

Fame itself isn't a bad thing. In fact, God calls some people to live in the public eye. God chooses them to reach people on a broad scale as they use their platform to tell the world about Jesus' love.

Their work isn't more important than the work of someone influencing one life at a time; it's just different. It all serves the same purpose. It all honors the same God who gives everyone distinct talents and opportunities to carry out His plan.

But sometimes we misuse the gifts God gives us. Rather than making Jesus famous, we seek to make ourselves famous. We lose any sense of *humility*—defined by dictionary.com as "a modest opinion of one's own importance"[6]—and instead grow prideful.

When this happens, our selfish ambitions distract us from God's purpose. We can get so hooked on people's applause and approval that we begin to chase the spotlight for all the wrong reasons.

Ultimately, our selfish ambitions can lead to our downfall. We might see our star rise and then crash when our pride leads to destruction (Proverbs 16:18). As author and speaker Christine Caine said, "If the light that is on you is brighter than the light that is in you, the light that is on you will destroy you."[7]

Nobody is immune to this temptation, which is why we must all be on guard. Each of us must know ourselves well enough to keep our hearts and our pride in check.

Even in ministry, people can get offtrack. Particularly in this age of Christian rock stars, where believers congregate in masses to praise Jesus, the people who lead those massive audiences must remember who the real star is.

It is all too easy to let praise and attention go straight to your head. It's easy to shift your loyalty from God to an audience of adoring fans who want to exalt you.

········•••••••··•••····•···•••···•··•••·· ♥ ·•••·····••··•••••··••··••••••··•••••··

God exalted him to the highest place and gave
him the name that is above every name, that
at the name of Jesus every knee should bow,
in heaven and on earth and under the earth.

—PHILIPPIANS 2:9-10

··•••··•••···•••••··•··•••···•··•••···•••··•••··•••··••···•••···••···•••···••••···•··

Keeping a Pure Heart

In the opening story, Samantha's desire for fame interfered with her call to serve God. Although she started out with godly intentions, she began to see her service to God as a way to advance her personal agenda.

She began to love God's power more than God Himself. She came to think of Him as a magic genie who could reward her for her good choices by making her dreams come true.

But God doesn't work like that. He doesn't bless the rule followers and block the rebels. No, God loves everyone equally all the time. His grace doesn't discriminate. And what pleases Him more than grand gestures and public proclamations are those intimate moments when you open your heart to Him, rest in His presence, and choose to totally trust Him.

God wants us to love Him, not use Him. And if your heart has any ulterior motives, He'll see them. You can't fool Him.

You might fool the world, however. What impresses the world can distance you from God, even as you serve Him, if your heart isn't in the right place.

You can have a heart full of Scripture—yet no heart for God.

You can be great at marketing Jesus—yet terrible at following Him.

You can be celebrated by adults as a role model for girls—yet disappoint God by taking too much pride in your moral record and thinking you're better than your peers, like Samantha did.

The goal of a Christian life is to have a heart on fire for Jesus. When you're passionate about Him, you lose ulterior motives. You trust God to lead you into your best life possible, and you show your trust by asking Him to align your heart and your dreams with His will so *your* desires for yourself match *His* desires for you.

Then, rather than asking, *What can God do for me?* you begin to ask, *What can I do for God?* You pray for God to give you wisdom and guidance.

Sometimes God will call you onstage to deliver a message to a crowd. Sometimes He'll keep you backstage. Sometimes He'll want you in the audience to cheer for others. And sometimes He'll assign you to direct or lead others.

Whatever you do, do it for God.

See your time in the spotlight as an opportunity to honor Jesus.

Consider moments of behind-the-scenes service as sweet opportunities to connect with Jesus.

Use your time in the audience to invest in your relationships and celebrate friends.

And approach your time in leadership as a chance to help others reach their potential.

Fame may seem like a big deal, but it's fleeting. Fame doesn't boost your standing before God, and it doesn't last for eternity. In heaven, there are no autograph lines. Celebrities don't get VIP perks or privileges that are denied to others.

So keep fame and fortune in perspective. Use your gifts and the opportunities God gives you to make an eternal difference, not a temporary splash. With faith as your guide, you can shine His light and live a life that honors Him.

···•·······•·•·······•·······•·•······· ♥ ·······•·•········•·•·•···•······•······•···

Use your gifts and the opportunities
God gives you to make an eternal
difference, not a temporary splash.

···•·······•·•·····•·•······•·•···•······•····•·······•···•···•······•·•·······•········•···

>>>— ••• ♡ ••• —<<<

Twenty Ways to Grow an Active Faith

There are *many* opinions about faith in this world. And if you listen to people who don't genuinely love God and live by His truths, they can mislead you.

Your spiritual journey is about you and your Creator. While others can lead you, teach you, and inspire you, human beings are flawed. We all get it wrong sometimes.

So if you're looking for the perfect role model, look to Jesus. Let Him be your ultimate example of faith.

Accepting Jesus as your Savior is the cornerstone of Christianity. In John 14:6, He said, "I am the way and the truth and the life. No one comes to the Father except through me." Whether you've begun your Christian journey, are contemplating it, or want to learn more about faith in Jesus, this section offers some key principles.

Christianity is less about *showing* you're a Christian and more about *growing* as a Christian. It's about devoting your life to God and letting Him transform you from the inside out.

As God works in you, you become a living witness to His grace and His love. You create a ripple effect for good by your character and your life.

Below are twenty ways to grow your Christian faith and cultivate a heart like Christ.

1. Make God the authority in your life. The first and primary commandment is to love God with all your heart, soul, and mind (Matthew 22:37–38). This means asking God for guidance and consulting Him about decisions like: *Are these friends good for me? How should I handle the school bully? What college is the best fit for me?*

Nobody loves you like God does! You're His masterpiece, after all. And while He will speak through your loved ones and the kind-hearted people you encounter, He longs for personal conversation with you. When you do talk, remember that He's a great counselor and adviser. After all, God sees your entire life story at once. He knows what you need *now* to be ready for *tomorrow.*

Psalm 16:2 (NLT) says, "I said to the LORD, 'You are my Master! Every good thing I have comes from you.'" Making God your authority is a declaration that you trust Him, that you recognize your blessings as gifts from Him, and that you seek His help to use those blessings wisely.

2. Walk in truth. In today's culture of "anything goes," there's no common moral code. People create their own truths to live by, and the world says it's okay.

But there's only one source of truth, and that is God because God *is* truth. Throughout Scripture God gives us a road map of truths to live by as well as guidelines for our good.

Just like toddlers being told, "It's okay to run in our backyard, but don't run into the street," we need boundaries that will keep us safe. We also need frequent reminders to use God's gifts the way He intends, for our ultimate good.

Verse 4 of 3 John says, "I have no greater joy than to hear that my children are walking in the truth." Everyone strays outside of God's parameters, but since God is merciful, He always welcomes us back and extends an open invitation to walk with Him and live by His truths.

3. Don't judge. As humans, we readily compare ourselves with others. We often downplay our shortcomings by comparing ourselves to people who seem like bigger messes than we are.

But the truth is, we're all messes. We're all sinners in need of a Savior because sin is sin, and no one sinner is better than another sinner. Nobody deserves God's blessings. As Romans 3:23 says, "All have sinned and fall short of the glory of God."

But God loves us anyway. He is patient and He sees our potential, so He constantly gives us second chances and new opportunities to seek Him.

The way you judge others is the way God judges you (Matthew 7:2). So, when judgmental thoughts come to mind, remember your own sinful ways, and respond to the mistakes of others with compassion and prayer.

4. Stay humble. Jesus was born a king, but on earth He didn't live like a king. He didn't hang out with the wealthiest people, live in a palace, or expect the world to kiss His feet.

In fact, Jesus did the opposite. He washed the feet of His disciples at the Last Supper (John 13). He lived a simple life as a carpenter's son, reached out to those who were ostracized by society, and spent His life serving others.

In Matthew 23:12, Jesus said, "Those who exalt themselves will be humbled, and those who humble themselves will be exalted." In a world where we worship celebrities and encourage self-promotion, this message is countercultural. But God's view of success turns our ideas upside down.

As you become more like Christ, you'll naturally become more humble. This is why the saints all talked about and recognized their sinfulness. Growing close to God heightens your awareness of how often you miss the mark. Only He can help you (and me) grow spiritually.

5. Let your life do the talking. Effective Christians don't need to tell people that they're Christians. People notice a difference in the way these individuals live and how they treat others.

What people are recognizing, consciously or not, is God's Spirit. When the Holy Spirit lives in you, you see people and life events differently.

God's Spirit makes you kinder, more loving, and slower to anger than the average person. It helps you forgive those who hurt you and pray for their hearts to soften. When your peers make bad choices and everyone is laughing at them or condemning them, you feel compassion and want to show love.

There's a time to share Scripture and a time to live Scripture. As 1 John 4:12 says, "No one has ever seen God; but if we love one another, God lives in us and his love is made complete in us." When you love others well, your faith speaks for itself.

6. Be patient. A relationship with God doesn't guarantee constant joy and big miracles. It truly is amazing to sense God's supernatural presence and to see His work in your life, but you'll also have seasons of doubt and possibly long dry spells when you don't see or feel God at all. These times call for patience.

When you are in a hard season or dry spell, you can hold on to the truth that God is there. He walks before you and with you (Deuteronomy 31:8). Your faith in God will grow when you trust Him in advance to carry you through a trial and then look back to see how faithful He was. God's ways are best understood when reflecting *back* on your life. Sometimes only then do the pieces of the puzzle make sense.

Our world has lost the art of patience because we're used to instant gratification. We want our heart's desires *now*. But what God has planned is worth the wait. Though His timing is a mystery, He works all things together for good for those who love Him (Romans 8:28).

7. Practice honest self-reflection. Some Christians are over-the-top passionate about telling others about Jesus. Evangelism done well is good and necessary, but focusing too intently on the spiritual condition of others can make you neglect the spiritual work that you need to do.

Mature Christians know that, and they look inward rather than judging other people. They "get real" and take an honest moral inventory, and such self-examination is tough. None of us likes to think about or admit our failings, struggles, fears, doubts, bad habits, ugly emotions, or baggage. Besides making us feel bad, these things usually trigger shame and guilt.

But God isn't looking to shame anyone. After all, nothing we realize about ourselves can change His love for us. God calls us to acknowledge and confess our sins so that He can set us free. He wants you to seek His forgiveness, receive it, and leave the past behind. You will be freer to serve Him.

Psalm 139:23–24 says, "Search me, God, and know my heart; test me and know my anxious thoughts. See if there is any offensive way in me, and lead me in the way everlasting."

Self-reflection leads to self-awareness, which enables you to see yourself through God's eyes and recognize your potential.

8. Tell people about God's work in your life. Have you ever met someone who impacts you significantly, and as you consider the wonderful things they've done for you, you feel a burning desire to tell someone?

Well, getting to know God is a lot like that. As you recognize His work in your life—how He saved you from a bad relationship, how He restored you during a broken time, how He protected you from an accident that you miraculously survived with only a cut on your hand—you'll naturally feel inclined to tell someone how real, powerful, and amazing He is.

Isaiah 63:7 says, "I will tell of the kindnesses of the LORD, the deeds for which he is to be praised, according to all the LORD has done for us." Sharing your story about the evidence you've seen of God helps build your faith and the faith of others. It reinforces our beliefs and gives us something tangible to cling to.

9. Choose joy. When God lives in your heart, it shows in your joyful spirit. You also radiate love and reveal a softness that disarms people and makes them feel comfortable.

The reason for a Christian's joy can be summed up in three words: *Christ is risen.* Because of Jesus, we have the hope of heaven. We understand pain on earth as temporary, and we can live for the promise of eternal life when there will be no more sorrow or pain.

First Peter 1:8 says, "Though you have not seen him, you love him; and even though you do not see him now, you believe in him and are filled with an inexpressible and glorious joy." Belief in a living God brings colors to a Christian's life. It creates a deep inner joy that is unaffected by changing circumstances because that joy is rooted in heaven.

10. Be generous with kindness and love. Most of us dole out kindness and love based on who we think deserves it, but God calls us to aim higher. He wants us to be kind and loving even when people don't deserve it, because that's how He treats us.

God's kindness leads to repentance (Romans 2:4). So if you

really want to live out your faith and give people a taste of the Lord's mercy, begin with kindness. Kindness truly is a universal love language.

11. Put your faith into action. Saying you're a Christian is simple. Adopting a Christian lifestyle—and the spiritual disciplines that go with it—takes commitment.

One reason why many people choose *not* to be a Christian is because they don't like the Christians they know. They're turned off when Christians say one thing, then do another. These onlookers are understandably put off by Christians who talk the talk but don't walk the walk.

True faith in Jesus leads to actions and behaviors that reflect your faith in Him and your love for Him. Though salvation comes from faith in Jesus—not hard work or good deeds—genuine love for Jesus will spur you to action. You'll *want* to do good things for God, not to earn brownie points or favor but as a way of sharing and responding to the blessings you've been given.

As God pours into you, you pour into others. You learn to live out the words of James 1:22 (ESV): "Be doers of the word, and not hearers only, deceiving yourselves." When you have a relationship with Jesus Christ, your faith will inevitably impact how you live.

12. Pursue virtue. Nobody lives a virtuous life by accident. Virtue is the habit of choosing what's good and right, and what results is a life of moral excellence.

Philippians 4:8 says, "Whatever is true, whatever is noble, whatever is right, whatever is pure, whatever is lovely, whatever is admirable—if anything is excellent or praiseworthy—think about such things."

Virtue is about holding high standards for your words, thoughts, and deeds—and recognizing God's grace as the force enabling you to live that way. Without grace, nobody can resist the pressures, temptations, and urges to stray from the way God wants us to live. And since nobody is perfect all the time, it's best to pursue virtue with prayer and lots of humility.

13. Unite with other believers. God promises that when two or three believers gather in His name, He is present with them (Matthew 18:20). You find strength and security in having like-minded friends who share your commitment to Him.

Christians are called to pour into each other, filling each other up with hope, joy, and courage, and then go our separate ways to live authentic lives.

However, Christians who talk only to other believers don't do much good for those who are seeking, lost, or unaware of God's love. God created us to be lights in the darkness, to take the blessings we receive in personal encounters and share them in a wider sphere of influence.

Uniting with kindred spirits helps you bravely serve God. No matter how the world receives you, you have core relationships you can count on, ones that empower you and keep you focused on what's important.

14. Practice gratitude. In 1 Thessalonians 5:18 (NLT), we are instructed to "be thankful in all circumstances, for this is God's will for you who belong to Christ Jesus."

The key phrase here is *in all circumstances*. While some blessings are obvious, others must be discovered. They're the hidden treasures that remind you God is good even when life is hard.

Your father may have lost his job, for instance, but you can be thankful that you still have him. Even as your dad searches for work, you can be thankful for your extra time together and little perks like having him pick you up from school.

Liked

Gratitude creates positive thoughts, and positive thoughts often lead to a more positive life. While this world says, "More is never enough," gratitude replies, "I have everything I need." Gratitude yields peace in your heart so you can thank God for the blessings you already have.

15. Listen for God's voice. Some people believe God doesn't talk to them. They think He plays favorites with the holy ones, who seem to hear Him and see Him so clearly.

But God talks to everyone. The problem isn't His lack of attention to us, but our lack of attention to Him. As Job 33:14 (NLT) says, "God speaks again and again, though people do not recognize it."

You may want God to make a dramatic entrance. Wouldn't it be great if He tapped you on the shoulder, spoke into your ear, and handed you a notebook with your whole life mapped out? Unfortunately, it doesn't work like that. Most often, God's voice is a quiet knowing that comes when you seek Him.

An active faith helps you recognize when God is at work in your life. As you introduce things into your life that He's told you to do—as you pray, serve, take care of people, refuse to judge, go to church, love sacrificially, read the Bible—you'll become more sensitive to His presence. You'll hear His voice not audibly, but instead as a deep certainty that specific ideas and thoughts you have are from Him and that you're meant to act on them.

God speaks differently to everyone. As you get to know Him better, you'll learn to hear His voice.

16. Be authentic. When it comes to loving Jesus, there's no cookie-cutter approach. No two believers are the same since God works uniquely in each unique person He has created.

In 1 Peter 4:10–11 (NLT), we are told that:

God has given each of you a gift from his great variety of spiritual gifts. Use them well to serve one another. Do you have the gift of speaking? Then speak as though God himself were speaking through you. Do you have the gift of helping others? Do it with all the strength and energy that God supplies. Then everything you do will bring glory to God through Jesus Christ. All glory and power to him forever and ever! Amen.

Rather than conform to what you believe a "good Christian" looks like, apply God's timeless truths to your authentic personality. Become the girl God created you to be because the real you reflects the real God.

17. Be brave in Jesus' name. Throughout your life, God will call you to serve in small ways and big ways. He'll stretch you beyond your comfort zone with every obedient yes.

Sometimes you'll feel overwhelmed. You may regret saying yes. And you may even believe that God picked the wrong girl for the job.

In these moments, remember 2 Timothy 1:6–7: "Fan into flame the gift of God, which is in you through the laying on of my hands. For the Spirit God gave us does not make us timid, but gives us power, love and self-discipline."

God makes you brave, not timid. He wants you to be passionate about Him and the jobs He created you to do. Even if you're unsure of yourself, you can be sure of Him. You can trust Him to lead the way.

18. See the world as your family. Every human being is made in God's image. He wants us to care for one another. As brothers and sisters in Christ, therefore, we should use our gifts to serve one another (Romans 12:5).

Helping others should be done quietly and without fanfare. As Jesus said in Matthew 6:3–4, "When you give to the needy, do not let your left hand know what your right hand is doing, so that your giving may be in secret. Then your Father, who sees what is done in secret, will reward you."

God wants you to love your brothers and sisters for Him, not for attention. Doing so not only strengthens the family unit, but it also strengthens you.

19. Know your enemy. You may think that your biggest enemy is the boy who just dumped you, the friend who betrayed you, or the teacher who doesn't get you.

The real force you're fighting, however, is Satan, the father of lies. He is your only true enemy (John 8:44).

John 10:10 says, "The thief comes only to steal and kill and destroy; I have come that they may have life, and have it to the full."

Satan takes pleasure in stirring up hate, rage, confusion, anxiety, and shame. He'll help you succeed at things that separate you from God. But don't be scared—Satan is powerless next to Jesus. So when you sense he may be at work, pull out your secret weapon: Jesus. Tell Satan to go away in the name of Jesus, and ask God to protect you from any future attacks.

20. Pray. Prayer is the anchor of a healthy spiritual life. No prayer is too small for God because He cares about every detail of your life.

You can pray and connect with God anywhere. Besides setting aside time in the morning or at night, you can send up a two-second prayer of praise or cry for help, something like *Help me ace this test I studied so hard for!* or *Thank You for this success—and help me stay humble!* or *Please give me the right words to say to my friend who is being mean.*

Prayer is especially important when you face temptation and need a way out. God has promised that He won't let you be tempted beyond what you can bear (1 Corinthians 10:13). So when you face any kind of temptation, pray. Ask God for the wisdom and the strength you need to bravely walk away.

········•·······•····•··•····•··•······ ♥ ······•··•···•··•··•··•···•··•··•··

When a man's ways please the Lord, he makes even his enemies to be at peace with him.

—PROVERBS 16:7 ESV

········•·······•··•···•··•··•·······•··•····•··•···•··•···•··•··•·······•··

He Died for You, So Why Not Live for Him?

Nobody arrives in heaven in a stretch limo.

Nobody takes a bank account or a trust fund to heaven.

Nobody enters heaven with an entourage of fans.

So while it may seem you have "arrived" if you achieve wealth and fame in this life, that view is shortsighted. Money and power are fleeting. They're inconsequential in the grand scheme of life. When your time on earth expires, you leave it all behind.

The flipside of that is, you're free from a lot of the daily pressures around you. You don't have to waste your time and energy chasing the world's idea of success.

While the world screams, "Shoot for the stars!" God whispers, "Aim higher! Aim for heaven! It will satisfy your heart's deepest desire."

As you keep your eyes on heaven, expect that God will give you God-sized dreams to pursue. Some may be so big that they scare you. You may fear you can't handle them—and the truth is, you can't handle them alone—but with God's help, you can. You have a partner who knows a thing or two about making miracles happen.

And as you use your gifts to serve God and pursue the dreams He has given you, keep any applause in perspective. Remember who the real star is and that your purpose is to help people know Him. The human heart is easily distracted, and all of us can relate to the words of John 12:43 (ESV): "For they loved the glory that comes from man more than the glory that comes from God."

Does it feel amazing to hear the sound of a crowd cheering for you? Of course it does! These moments remind you that you're noticed, seen, and appreciated.

But a crowd's applause is temporary. It comes in short-lived spurts. And if that applause is your primary motivation for anything you're doing, you'll exhaust yourself trying to earn it, and you'll be frustrated when someone else gets the applause, replacing you as the crowd's favorite.

The better way to live is to let Jesus be the star. Listen to God, accept the supporting roles He calls you to, and keep a heart of humility. Besides strengthening your faith, this will lead you to long-lasting peace.

Jesus died for you, so why not live for Him? Why not pursue dreams that will keep you pursuing God? Imagine that moment when you meet your Maker face-to-face and hear Him say about your life, "Well done, good and faithful servant! . . . Come and share your master's happiness!" (Matthew 25:23).

It's one thing to shoot for the stars—and it's quite another to aim for heaven. Decide now which goal you're aiming for, and let your life reflect it.

♥

While the world screams, "Shoot for the stars!" God whispers, "Aim higher! Aim for heaven! It will satisfy your heart's deepest desire."

✦ Discussion Questions ✦

1. On a scale of one to ten, how important is fame to you? Explain why it is or isn't so important to you.

2. Are you more likely to think, *What can God do for me?* or *What can I do for God?* What does your honest answer tell you about yourself?

3. What part of the Christian lifestyle—such as praying, serving, taking care of people, refusing to judge, going to church, loving sacrificially, reading the Bible—seems the hardest to practice? Why?

4. What would happen if girls stopped treating each other as competition and instead united for God? In what ways would relationships change?

5. What is the difference between a humble heart and a prideful heart? When has pride ever gotten the best of you? How would you handle that same situation if it happened again today?

6. What three steps can you take to activate or deepen your faith?

9

Courage

 You were made to change the world.
Don't let the world change you.

$\mathcal{E}$very day at school Adeline felt pressure that wasn't related to her schoolwork or her activities.

The pressure came from her friends who liked to run her life. Again and again they told Adeline what she needed to do, as if her life depended on their guidance.

You need to buy these jeans.

You need to drive this car.

You need to date boys in this group.

You need to shop at this store.

After two years of hearing her friends tell her "You need to," Adeline had reached her limit. She was tired of the constant advice and being treated like a puppet who wasn't capable of making choices for herself.

From an outsider's perspective, Adeline probably seemed lucky. She was part of the popular crowd, and that automatically elevated her status.

But what people failed to see were the rules and expectations of this particular crowd. Belonging came with strings attached, and Adeline was constantly under scrutiny as her friends dictated what she should do, say, and wear.

Once, when she tried to be different by wearing a funky hat, her friends teased her and said she looked ridiculous. They told her to stick with classic brands because the Bohemian look wasn't *her*. But who were they to make that call? How did they know what look best suited her?

The worst part was, Adeline listened to these friends. She never wore that hat again because every time she put it on, their voices rang in her head.

Adeline wished she didn't care so much about what these girls thought, but she did. Having their approval made everyone at school treat her special, and if she lost their friendships, she would lose that special treatment too.

Besides, it wasn't *all bad* being their friend. These girls were funny, and they always planned fun outings. On a good day Adeline could forget the negatives. She could overlook those things that drove her nuts.

But on the bad days—which increasingly outnumbered the good days—Adeline wondered if their friendships were worth it. She also wondered if every friend group had endless rules and suggestions about what people needed to fix about themselves.

What hurt Adeline most, however, was how these girls dismissed her love for art. Convinced that all the artists at their school were "too eccentric," they told Adeline to keep her passion under wraps. But why have a passion if you can't share it? And why was Adeline dumb enough to be dragged into taking dance classes with her friends when she didn't even like to dance?

Adeline was reaching a breaking point. The friendships she'd long considered a blessing had become a curse.

While she liked being in the popular crowd, she still felt lonely and unsatisfied. All the changes she'd made to fit in with that circle, and all the time she'd spent pretending to be someone she wasn't, had totally messed with her head.

At this point Adeline was so accustomed to being told what to do that she wasn't sure what *she* wanted anymore.

Was there a way out? Could she find a place of acceptance without losing herself? If Adeline cut ties with these girls, would it be the end of a social life for the rest of high school? Or would it be a new beginning, a chance to start over and be true to herself at last?

❤

"I will go before you and make
the rough places smooth."

—ISAIAH 45:2 NASB

Who Is Shaping You?

One of the greatest urges you're likely to face in life is the urge to be like everyone else.

Chances are, you've felt this pressure already. You've been shaped, molded, and influenced by the people, the events, and the patterns in your immediate environment.

It's natural to become more like the people you spend the majority of your time with. Whatever subculture you're exposed to will inevitably rub off on you.

This is why you may act and talk like your peers at school.

Dress like your closest friends.

Obsess over the same celebrities, TV shows, and musicians you hear everyone raving about.

And even imitate the girls who get the most attention.

Having things in common with your friends and acquaintances

Liked

is good. Without some common ground, what would you talk about, share, and dream about together?

At the same time, there's a hidden risk to every subculture because it can distance you from who you're meant to be. With every group comes a subtle pressure to conform and the temptation to follow the crowd in order to fit in.

Sometimes conformity is beneficial. Conforming to the rules and laws of society, for instance, cultivates peace, order, and harmony. Conforming to and being shaped by positive influences helps you grow and become a better person.

But when conformity goes against your better instincts or God's best for you, it stops being good. It stunts rather than supports your growth.

Like Adeline in the opening story, you may feel torn. You may experience inner tension as you're pulled in a direction that doesn't feel right and you try to reconcile your desire to fit in with your need to be your own person.

God made you unique *on purpose*. He created you to live authentically as you, not identically to other girls. And believe it or not, your differences are a gift. They are part of God's plan for you, allowing you to serve your generation like no one in the universe has ever served before.

God didn't create you to be a carbon copy of anyone else. He doesn't want you hiding, ignoring, or downplaying your deepest thoughts and feelings. Your personality, passions, and preferences distinguish you from the crowd. Who you are reveals God's creativity in a unique, unprecedented, and unrepeatable way.

Even so, it's hard to let your differences show. It can be scary to admit that you're not exactly like everyone else and risk an uncertain reaction.

But can I tell you what's even worse, my friend? Not being the person God created you to be and missing out on the opportunities

140

God has planned for you because you've settled for less than His best. Unfortunately, some people might have you believe that the ultimate accomplishment for a girl is to become one of the following:

- ♡ The most popular, the most beautiful, or the best-dressed girl in school.
- ♡ The most "liked" girl on social media.
- ♡ A viral sensation.
- ♡ A rich superstar.
- ♡ The center of attention.
- ♡ The object of every boy's attention.

Before you let anyone push these goals on you, however, I encourage you to think about them. Imagine what God's response might be if these were your highest aspirations.

I imagine Him whispering, "Aim higher. Dream bigger. You were made for so much more. Don't let the obsessions of this world distract you from My plan."

You were born to make an eternal difference. You have a God who adores you in all your uniqueness and who wants you to show *more* of your true self, not *less*.

And while the world wants its way with you—hoping to mold you into its idea of female perfection—God wants you to embrace yourself as the one-of-a-kind person you are. He plans to empower you through Christ to live a one-of-a-kind life.

Life's highest calling is not to become an Instagram Phenomenon, The Next Big Thing, or The Perfect Girl. No, life's highest calling is to live bravely and boldly for Jesus. When the One who walked on water walks with you, miracles can happen. With Him you can find the freedom to chart your own course and the courage to chase a life that is unique and deeply satisfying.

Liked

Life's highest calling is not to become an Instagram Phenomenon, The Next Big Thing, or The Perfect Girl. No, life's highest calling is to live bravely and boldly for Jesus.

Quick Quiz: Are You a Leader or a Follower?

Imagine it's that time of year again—time to choose your schedule for the next school year. Already you feel the stress of trying to determine the right mix of classes.

Your friends are brilliant, so they load up on Advanced Placement (AP) classes. They encourage you to do the same, assuring you that a long list of AP courses will look good on college admission and scholarship applications.

But what your friends don't understand is how hard you have to work to keep up in these courses. You also have other commitments—like show choir and softball—that your friends don't have because school is their sole focus.

This year you took three AP classes. The workload kept you up past midnight most nights doing homework. You don't want to make that mistake again. Besides losing sleep, you almost lost your mind.

Yet here you are now, doubting your decision to lighten your load because your friends say that getting off the AP track may hurt you down the road.

What do you do?

A) You seek the advice of your parents and the school counselor to see what they think. You also pray about it. You ask God for wisdom, for the ability to discern what's best for *you,* and for confidence about your choices regardless of what your friends choose.

B) You take your friends' advice and stay on the AP track with all advanced classes. Although you know this will be a nightmare, you figure you'll deal with it and come up with a way to cope.

C) You cut yourself a break and sign up for the easiest classes possible. You've had enough stress and given yourself enough challenges. From now on, you'll only do things that require minimal effort.

D) You prioritize what's most important to you. Since you love math and French, you stay in these advanced classes. In all other subjects you take regular classes, which still creates a demanding schedule but won't completely exhaust you and leave you no room to breathe.

If you answered A or D, you're on the right track. You're praying to God, you're willing to seek wise counsel from trusted adults, and you're thinking for yourself in an attempt to strike a healthy balance in your life.

Making wise and healthy choices—choices that take into account your strengths, limitations, and personal realities—trains you to become a leader. It teaches you to consider options, pioneer your own path, and respect others who do the same.

Trusting God's Design for You

I'd like to let you in on a secret that may surprise you.

And that is, everyone feels like an outsider at times. Everyone questions whether they belong. Everyone knows the feeling of looking around a room and thinking, *What am I doing here? I have nothing in common with anyone.*

Maybe you've found your peeps, your tribe, or your squad. Your group is so tight, you call yourself family. You love and build one another up. You're certain you'll be friends for life.

Yet even in a dream scenario like this, you'll still have moments when you feel different or disconnected. You may have days—even months—in which loneliness, isolation, or insecurity seeps into your relationships.

Like when your friends all have prom dates, and you don't.

Or when your friends all have college plans in place, and you're still waiting to find out whether you've been accepted.

Or when your friends all have a terrific family life, and your parents are divorced and barely speaking to each other.

The point is, your life will never match anyone else's life. It will never live up to the romanticized (and totally unrealistic) ideals that magazines, movies, social media, and pop culture project as "the good life."

But please remember this: your life isn't a mistake just because it looks different from what you see around you, planned, or hoped for. You're not an outsider just because you feel like a misfit. Your future isn't hopeless just because your current situation seems bleak.

God is in control. He works all things together for good for those who love Him (Romans 8:28). God also promises that His plans for you are good so your future is promising: "I know the plans I have for you," declares the LORD, "plans to prosper you and not to harm you, plans to give you hope and a future" (Jeremiah 29:11).

You can trust God because God is trustworthy. He lets nothing that happens in your life go to waste. While the world likes to tell you, "Be tough. Keep up your guard. Don't let anyone see you sweat," God says, "Be softhearted. You're safe with Me. You can be vulnerable in My care because I understand you. I'm shaping you into a new creation."

Like a potter with clay, God wants to mold you, and He will treasure you as the work of His hands (Isaiah 64:8). And when you lean into His hands and allow Him to smooth out your rough edges and hold you close during life's tough seasons, you will know peace. Even if you can't pinpoint the direction He's moving you in, all will be well with your soul.

I encourage you to trust that feeling of peace because God is preparing you to be a world changer. He is teaching you to trust the Holy Spirit inside of you so He can equip you for your mission.

So be confident about your unique God-given design. And be respectful of the unique design He gave others. People have different personalities, passions, and preferences for a reason, and the best way to approach people who seem different from you is with a spirit of love and unity.

After all, beneath our obvious differences, we all have a lot in common.

We all have dreams and fears.

Strengths and weaknesses.

Days when we rock it and days when we lose it.

And a deep-rooted desire to be part of something bigger than ourselves.

So champion your friends and the people you encounter. Give them permission to be themselves, and find ways to work together.

Let your differences lead to growth, not division. Open your heart to God's presence, and then look for Him in unlikely places.

·· •·····•··•·····•··•·····•··•····· ♥ ·····•··•·····•··•·····•··•·····•·· ··

There is one God, the Father, by whom all things were created, and for whom we live. And there is one Lord, Jesus Christ, through whom all things were created, and through whom we live.

—1 CORINTHIANS 8:6 NLT

·· •·····•··•·····•··•·····•··•·····•··•·····•··•·····•··•·····•··•·····•·· ··

>>>- ••• ♡ ••• -<<<

Eight Ways to Become a World Changer

There are a million ways to become a world changer. The path differs for each person because God is infinitely creative.

But what unites change agents across the globe are both passion and purpose. Passion leads to purpose, and purpose leads to impact.

Here are eight ways to grow as a world changer and carve out a path that's right for you.

1. Recognize what your heart begs to do. What excites you? What are you drawn to and insanely curious about? What could you talk about all day and never get bored?

Your answers to these questions offer clues about your passions. If you're an avid fan of *Food Network,* for instance, and love watching the celebrity chefs, God may be grooming you for a food-related career.

If you love weddings and spend hours pinning party inspiration on Pinterest, you may be destined for a job as a wedding planner or an event coordinator.

Your passions and interests aren't random or coincidental. God wired you with certain talents and desires in hopes that you'll use your gifts for Him. Sometimes your passion may precede your talent. You may love tennis, yet you're not very good. People may discourage you or tell you to quit because they don't think it's your thing.

My advice is to keep going. Trust your instincts and chase those dreams that make you jump out of bed in the morning. If you love something enough, you'll work hard at it. And if you're not sure you're making the right commitment, talk to your parents or a trusted adult. Ask them to name the strengths they see in you, and discuss with them how your passions might fit with those strengths.

2. Worry less about what people think. One reason why girls don't chase their dreams is because they don't want to be criticized. Particularly in today's culture, when some people seem to enjoy attacking others, putting yourself out there can feel risky.

But living in fear holds you back from pursuing your dreams. It causes you to play it safe by never taking chances or leaving your comfort zone.

One day you'll regret this. Fifteen years from now, you'll kick yourself for not seizing an opportunity or following after an idea that excited you because you were afraid of what others might say or think.

The people who intimidate you now most likely won't be in your life in fifteen years. If they are and if they still act the same way, you'll feel sorry for them instead of feeling threatened by them. By then you'll have a different perspective and the ability to see how deeply insecure they are.

Real confidence comes from Jesus. His unconditional and never-changing love for you gives you a calm assurance that frees you from needing anyone's validation or approval. You and Jesus are a team, and when you take a risk with Him, you have nothing to fear.

3. Give yourself time. It's okay if you haven't identified any passions or dreams yet. It's okay to have no clue what you're meant to do.

God is writing a story with your life, and you're still at the beginning of that story. Right now God is planting seeds, introducing characters, and setting up the action. Events that seem inconsequential now may gain relevance later as the plot unfolds.

The best thing to do, then, is trust God. Let Him use your seasons of waiting—times when you have more questions than answers, more doubts than certainties—to strengthen your faith and build your character.

It's tempting to turn to the world for answers, especially when you get tired of waiting, but God wants you to turn to Him instead. Your seasons of waiting are great opportunities to grow in faith and trust God's plan instead of rushing it.

4. Be an original. Two things that can kill your quest for an authentic and meaningful life are comparison and envy.

Why? Because these two pitfalls mess with your mind. They lead you to use other girls as your yardstick and believe you're a failure when you don't measure up.

Remember, your life isn't supposed to look like anyone else's life. You're an original, not a replica. While it's good to have people who inspire you, their inspiration should be a starting point for your transformation, not your final destination.

When you were young, you were distinctly original. You didn't know how to be anyone but yourself. As you seek to be an original now, remember your younger self. Tap into that little girl, the one who was busy exploring the things that made her happy and blissfully unaware of how to cater to the world's expectations.

5. Be smart about what you consume. What goes into your mind influences your thoughts, actions, and habits. It creates a vision for what you believe your life should look like.

I know you like to chill out, and I understand that your brain needs a break from the pressures of life. But if you spend all your free time obsessing over celebrities or binge-watching shows on Netflix, your values will get distorted. You'll become more like your favorite idols and television characters and less like yourself.

Television shows are intentionally written with dramatic and juicy plots that lure you in. Pictures of celebrities are Photoshopped to make them look flawless and thinner than they really are.

None of what you see is real, so before you buy into the lies— and aim to meet those standards—put them through a filter. Use your knowledge about God to decide whether what you see in the media is a good life or a misguided life. Fill up on things that enrich your mind instead of numbing it and that create a strong vision for your life.

6. Surround yourself with good people. Part of figuring yourself out is knowing who to trust. Since different people bring out different sides of you, it's often hard to figure out who sees the real you.

While one friend says, "You're so loud! Your voice gives me a headache!" another friend may tell you, "You're so funny! My stomach hurts from laughing!"

Naturally this leaves you wondering: *Which friend is right? Who should I listen to? Should I tone down my personality, or is it okay to keep making people laugh? Which option is better? Which option is me?*

There are no right answers to questions like these, but there are other questions that may help you decide whether or not the company you keep is helping you grow in a good direction:

- *Do the people I hang out with like me, or are they always trying to change me?*
- *Do I like who I am when I'm around them?*
- *Do they bring out the best in me?*
- *Do they see the good in me?*
- *Do I feel secure in our relationship, or do I know that—given the right set of circumstances—they wouldn't hesitate to ditch me?*
- *Do they appreciate me, or do they act like they do me a favor by being my friend?*

New York Times bestselling author Bob Goff has said, "People grow where they're accepted."[8] So to become a world changer, surround yourself with friends who feed your soul rather than crush it.

After all, soul crushers are toxic. They cause grief, anxiety, stress, and sometimes even physical symptoms like stomachaches and headaches.

You can look out for yourself and set boundaries with soul crushers in ways that are still kind. Choosing uplifting friends is good for your emotional well-being, and you'll avoid those relationship dynamics that stunt your growth and trigger insecurity.

7. Make use of your strengths. God will equip you with everything you need to do His will. This means you don't have to be a bona fide superstar to begin serving Him.

Isn't that great news? Isn't it comforting to know that God uses ordinary people to do extraordinary things? What matters most isn't the talent you bring to the table, but rather how willing and teachable your heart is.

If you're open to doing God's will and brave enough to say, "Use me however You want," He will work through you to be a positive influence on others.

All around you, people have needs. They're experiencing loss, injustice, and unbearable pain. So think about the best use of your energy, time, and talents. Ask God to show you where to take the gifts and resources He's given you and how to effectively share them with others.

8. Find a mission. The secret to having a meaningful life is fixing your eyes on eternity. Now is the time to decide what you're living for and intentionally seek to become more like Christ.

Finding a mission that captivates your heart can point you in the right direction. Whatever you're drawn to, whatever troubles you, whatever you desperately want to see changed—that could be your mission field. It's very likely that God is stirring your heart and nudging you to move forward in His name as part of His plan.

Whenever you're ready, God can start using you as a world changer. All He needs is your yes and your willingness to make an eternal difference for Him.

········•··•·····•··•·····•··•·····•··•···· ❤ ·····•··•·····•··•·····•··•·····•··•····

Your life isn't supposed to look like anyone else's life. You're an original, not a replica.

········•··•·····•··•·····•··•·····•··•·····•··•·····•··•·····•··•····

Only God

There's no particular uniform you need to wear to serve God.

There's no one place you need to live to share the news about Jesus' love.

There's no specific friend group or social scene you have to be part of to live your best life possible.

Most of all, there's no one you need to listen to more than the One who made you.

This world will try to corner you and shape you according to its mold. It will press its opinions on you and present a narrow view of your options. Even well-meaning friends may pretend to be experts on you. They may sound convincing and completely sure of themselves.

But the truth is, only God is the expert on you. Only God has known since the beginning of time who you are, why you exist, and what you were born to do.

So before you face the world, let God make you firm in who you are and confident enough in your identity that you won't change for the wrong reasons.

God needs world changers everywhere—in schools, coffee shops, theaters, band rooms, chess clubs, gymnasiums, businesses, homes, dance studios, restaurants—the list is endless. So wherever He leads you, trust that He has a reason. Know you can make a difference wherever you are by choosing to walk with Jesus and drawing your strength from Him.

You're alive today for a reason. You've been equipped to serve your Creator. You can make unique contributions to the world, and with the help of God, you can embrace a life of authenticity that is right for you, pleasing to Him, and deeply satisfying for your soul.

Courage

Whether we are at home or away, we
make it our aim to please him.

—2 CORINTHIANS 5:9 ESV

Liked

❧ Discussion Questions ❧

1. When, if ever, have you not been truly yourself in order to fit in? How did it make you feel?

2. Name three things that make you unique. Are you proud of these differences or embarrassed by them? Why?

3. When, if ever, have you buried or at least ignored a passion because you were scared of failure or criticism? What passion(s) currently in your heart would you most like to pursue?

4. Write down two or three life goals you have. Are these goals that will make an eternal difference or a temporary splash?

5. Have you had to trust God during a time when He seemed silent? What was that experience like? Does your faith grow stronger or falter as you wait for answers and guidance?

6. Why does having a clear sense of purpose improve your quality of life?

10

Direction

 At the end of the day, only two questions matter: *Am I pleasing God?* and *Do I like who I'm becoming?*

It had been a stressful day at school—a stressful week, actually—and Gabrielle was glad it was over.

For several nights she'd tossed and turned in bed, never really falling asleep.

What kept popping up in Gabrielle's mind was a saying she once saw on a handmade pillow in an antique store. As Gabrielle struggled to sleep, trying to relax and calm her mind, this saying ran through her head:

A clear conscience is the softest pillow.

Gabrielle knew what was bothering her, but she wasn't sure how to fix it. Because right now, her friends were ecstatic. They had all celebrated her win for two weeks.

As the first female president of her school's Student Government Association, Gabrielle was a heroine. Her victory in the school election was considered a victory for every girl at Parker High School, and they all seemed to enjoy their new bragging rights.

After all, Gabrielle beat Drew Pearson, their class president since seventh grade. It had been a tight race and an intense campaign, and with most boys backing Drew and most girls behind Gabrielle, no one knew who would get the swing votes needed to win.

Gabrielle won by a narrow margin of seven ballots. When Drew and his campaign team demanded a recount, the tally stood.

Beating Drew gave Gabrielle tremendous satisfaction. He was so arrogant, and after he had pulled some low punches—like making up stories about Gabrielle's character and calling her unfit for leadership—Gabrielle was determined to show him up.

Gabrielle had every intention of winning fair and square, but when an opportunity to help her tally presented itself, she took it. On election day, an office aide who had a crush on Gabrielle told her that fourteen voters had completed their ballots and turned them in without voting for president. He offered to mark her name on those blank ballots if she wanted.

It seemed like a good plan when he texted Gabrielle with the idea, and she responded with a thumbs-up. After all, Drew deserved to lose—and she felt certain he'd do the same if he had the chance.

But two days after the election, Gabrielle's conscience kicked in. The trigger was a local newspaper reporter who asked Gabrielle to describe how she felt when she heard the final results.

"I was thrilled," Gabrielle replied, which was partially true. She loved watching the reaction around her as girls shrieked and jumped for joy.

What Gabrielle didn't admit was the nausea she felt when she learned she'd won by seven votes. Remembering the fourteen ballots rigged in her favor, she knew she didn't technically win.

Gabrielle was president only because she'd cheated. As easy

as it was to smile at school and thank everyone who congratulated her, the truth caught up with her when she tried to sleep at night. It bothered Gabrielle that she'd compromised her values. She had never cheated on anything before.

The worst part was, from the start Gabrielle didn't even like being president. Having everyone sharing their opinions with her and complaining about minor issues was stressful.

The problem wasn't Gabrielle's gender, but rather her personality: Gabrielle liked everyone to get along, and with a committee full of people with strong personalities and equally strong opinions, she was already dealing with more drama than she had bargained for.

Maybe this was normal. Maybe every leader faced similar challenges. Deep down, however, Gabrielle knew she was to blame. The reason her victory felt wrong was because it *was* wrong. She'd messed with the natural order of events, and this anguish was the price she'd have to pay.

A clear conscience is the softest pillow. Now Gabrielle definitely understood what this meant. The guilt was eating her alive. Gabrielle was losing sleep, sanity, and peace of mind. She hated who she had become.

On the other hand, she had a lot to lose by being honest and announcing that Drew was the rightful winner. Girls would be disappointed. Her family would be embarrassed. And Gabrielle would go down in history as the president who was disgraced.

But even the best day at school can't make up for the worst night in bed. Gabrielle had learned this firsthand. What happened when the lights went down and Gabrielle's conscience woke up forced her to confront the lie she had begun to live.

Gabrielle knew she had to make things right regardless of the consequences.

Direction

> "I am leaving you with a gift—peace of mind and heart. And the peace I give is a gift the world cannot give. So don't be troubled or afraid."
>
> **—JOHN 14:27** NLT

A Life That Pleases God

Planted deep inside of you is the desire to please God.

God wired you to live for Him, and through the Holy Spirit, He enables you to do so by helping you know what is true, good, and right.

Living a life that pleases God gives you a peaceful heart. When your life doesn't please Him, you feel friction instead of peace.

Throughout your life you'll experience times of peace _and_ times of friction. You'll feel torn, confused, and frustrated as you make good choices and poor choices, choices that align with God's design for you and choices that conflict with it.

It's natural to want to hide your face and run from God when you get it wrong, but He wants you to do the opposite. He wants you to run _to_ Him.

Why? Because God's power is made perfect in weakness (2 Corinthians 12:9). And when you mess up or hit rock bottom, you have an opportunity to encounter God's powerful grace, redemption, forgiveness, mercy, and love.

In the New Testament, the Greek word for _sin_ means "to miss the mark."[9] And while God certainly has high standards, He knows you'll miss the mark again and again.

Even your best days won't be sin-free. That's not because you're

159

a terrible person or because you lack willpower, but because sin is part of the human condition and a matter we all deal with.

The good news is, we have Jesus, who came down from heaven to save sinners. Through His death on the cross, your sins can be forgiven. God can redeem your mistakes and even bring good from them.

When God created you, He gave you a conscience to help you please Him. Your conscience is your innate sense of right and wrong; it is a moral compass intended to steer you toward Him. As you listen to your conscience and follow the lead of the Holy Spirit—as well as Scripture—it offers clarity into His plan, will, and wisdom.

Many people, however, treat their conscience as their enemy. They fight it and deliberately try to silence it.

But the truth is, your conscience is a gift. It can protect you from self-destruction. If mistakes and poor choices felt good, why would you ever stop?

Why would you ever choose a life with God if living life without God brought sustainable peace and happiness?

In the opening story, Gabrielle faced a crisis of conscience. A mistake that stayed dormant all day long suddenly consumed her mind at night. This is often how a conscience works. When your guard is down and you're alone with your thoughts, the truth tends to come out.

If you were in a situation like Gabrielle's, what do you believe would be the best thing to do? Would you take your secret to the grave, or would you come clean?

As you'd probably guess, God would want you to admit your mistake and tell the parties involved, "I messed up, and I'm so sorry. I'm willing to face the consequences of my mistake. I'll do whatever I can to right this wrong."

Does a confession like this take courage? Absolutely.

Are there people who might hold a mistake like this against you? Yes.

But even if that happens, you can't worry about those people because a life that pleases God is faithful to the truth. When you do the right thing, you are choosing to trust God to carry you through hard circumstances and the difficult consequences of your mistake. He will ultimately bless your decision to confess your sin, make the situation right, and deal with the consequences.

Pleasing God isn't about keeping a perfect track record and never messing up. If that were the case, none of us would stand a chance!

More than a squeaky-clean résumé, God desires your heart. He wants you so deeply engaged with Him and attuned to your spiritual desires that you naturally draw closer to Him by:

♡ *Spending time with Him.*
♡ *Learning about Him.*
♡ *Reading and studying the Bible.*
♡ *Sharing God's love.*
♡ *Resisting temptation.*
♡ *Admitting your sins.*
♡ *Facing the consequences of poor choices.*
♡ *Forgiving others.*
♡ *Seeking His counsel on both big matters and small ones.*
♡ *Making Him the center of your life.*
♡ *Honoring Him with your thoughts, words, and deeds.*

If this list sounds overwhelming, remember that loving God isn't about checking off tasks. It's not meant to be burdensome or stressful. God wants you as you are, where you are, and whenever you're ready to talk. When you come close to Him, He'll come close to you (James 4:8).

So go to God with no underlying motive and no desire to be anyone but yourself. *You're enough just the way you are.* When you're in His presence, your beauty is magnified. You have the glow of a girl who knows she is loved and who finds her security in the One who always welcomes her company.

···•·········•·······•···•·······•····•···· ♥ ···•·····•····•···•·•···•···•···•···•···

Those who look to him are radiant; their
faces are never covered with shame.

—PSALM 34:5

···•·······•····•···•···•···•···•·•···•···•···•···•···•···•···•···•···•··

Living with Meaningful Direction

One of the best parts of pleasing God is how it helps you like yourself.

When you live according to your God-given design and the truths you innately know (Romans 2:14–15), you'll be able to experience a deeper peace and joy than anything the world offers.

It's dangerous to let yourself be consumed by what other people think of you (Proverbs 29:25). It's shortsighted and unhealthy to seek validation from others and base your self-worth on temporary measures like:

♡ How often people praise you.
♡ How many friends you have.
♡ How many invitations you receive.
♡ How popular you are on social media.
♡ How much positive feedback you hear.

The truth is, you can be applauded by the world, yet be miserable inside.

You can be worshipped for your appearance, yet hate the skin you're in.

You can fool everyone into believing that you always have your act together, yet suffer in silence because it really is an act.

The applause you crave most isn't the kind that rocks stadiums, but the kind that rocks your heart. The applause that truly satisfies your soul is the quiet whisper of God that tells you you're on the right track and that He is pleased with you because you are seeking Him.

Applause like this is also called *peace*. It frees you to sleep at night. It allows you to feel good about yourself. It brings comfort even in hard times and satisfies your deep desire to live a meaningful life.

And that desire will impact the direction you choose for your life. Although you're young, you're headed toward eternity. You're making choices daily that set a trajectory for your life. *And if your choices don't draw you closer to God, they'll slowly carry you away from Him.*

To determine if your life has a positive trajectory, ask yourself these questions:

♡ *Do I like where I'm going?*
♡ *Am I making good choices that will lead to opportunities and open doors down the road, or am I making poor choices that will hurt me and ultimately close doors?*
♡ *Are my best friends on a positive path? Do they enrich my life?*
♡ *Do I pour time and energy into things—like building people up— that have eternal significance? Will my legacy outlive my time on earth?*
♡ *Do I show integrity and character in all that I say and do?*
♡ *Do I like who I'm becoming? Am I a better person today than I was a year ago? If not, what steps can I take to become a better person?*

That last question deserves special attention. The key word is *becoming*. When God looks at you, He sees who you're *becoming*. He looks beyond the mistakes, setbacks, and challenges in your life that discourage you.

Where your life is going matters tremendously to God. Even baby steps of progress make His heart sing because one step in the right direction means you're one step closer to Him.

Whether you're biting your tongue so you don't yell at your brother or planning to admit a big mistake, God rejoices. He is proud of you because He knows that the right choice is often the hard choice.

God knows your entire life story, and the best chapters are yet to come. So please don't ever give up on yourself—and don't ever give up on God. His power is so much greater than any trial you face, and in His perfect time, He can restore anything.

A life that pleases God shapes you into the image of Christ. So fix your eyes on that goal, and let God lead you in a direction that honors Him and gives you inner peace.

♥

When God looks at you, He sees who you're *becoming*. He looks beyond the mistakes, setbacks, and challenges in your life that discourage you.

A Life That Leads You Home

Nobody can make you love God.

Nobody can force you into a relationship with God.

Nobody can grow your faith for you. You can't piggyback on someone else's faith instead of building your own.

The truth is, faith is every individual's personal choice and a matter of the heart. Only *you* can decide whether to commit your life to God. Only *you* can let your desire to please Him overwhelm your desire to please or impress other people.

Growing closer to God isn't a smooth, effortless process. At times it gets messy, complicated, and challenging.

You may take two steps forward, then one step back.

Or you may wake up one day and realize you've not just drifted away from who you're meant to be, but that you are altogether lost. More than ever before, you want to return home.

Home to your roots.

Home to your safe place.

Home to what feels familiar and right.

The good news is, God will rescue you. He'll show up whenever you call to Him, and He'll reveal a better way. But first you must realize—in your heart as well as your mind—that any homesickness you feel is more than a yearning for family, friends, or even an old zip code.

It's a yearning for *Him*.

You yearn for God because He created you for heaven. You were designed to live in a close relationship with Him. And while it's impossible to know perfect peace this side of heaven, you can experience the deepest peace known to man—the peace that surpasses all understanding and protects your heart and mind (Philippians 4:7).

God is waiting to give you the best He has to offer. He has a plan for your life that will bring you peace on earth and eternal rewards.

His rewards are worth the wait. So is your long journey home. You have been created to go the distance, to take this one life you've been given, rise up to your full potential, and develop the confidence, courage, and ability to like yourself—regardless of what anyone else thinks.

Liked

············· ♥ ·············

You, LORD, give perfect peace to
those who keep their purpose firm
and put their trust in you.

—ISAIAH 26:3 GNT

·····································

❦ Discussion Questions ❧

1. When have you lost sleep because of a mistake you made? What, if anything, did you do to make the situation right?

2. On a scale of one to ten, how much importance do you place on pleasing God? Why did you answer with that number?

3. Do you like who you're becoming? Why or why not?

4. What three habits can you adopt to take your life in a more meaningful direction?

5. Does the idea of living for God's approval make you feel stressed or relieved? Explain why.

6. When has God rescued you from a difficult circumstance? Describe the situation, what God did, and how that experience affected your faith.

Conclusion

One crucial component of living a happy, healthy, positive life is to let go of unrealistic ideas.

One of those ideas is to believe it's possible to make *everybody* like you.

The truth is, some people will never like you. No matter what you do or say, you'll never win them over or gain their approval.

I say this not to discourage you, but to set you free. Much of the time, the problem is theirs. Their hearts are too hard, too small, or too cynical to see the good in you, and rather than give you the benefit of the doubt, they automatically assume the worst.

When you're friendly, they call you fake.

When you're quiet, they call you aloof.

When you're energetic, they call you intense.

And when you're winning, they call you lucky or overrated.

The good news is, you don't need mass approval to live a spectacular life. You don't need a majority vote to carry out God's special mission for you.

Our God is a God of miracles, and when He wants a job done, He'll move heaven and earth to make it happen. Even the most powerful and influential individual you know can't thwart what the good Lord has in mind.

It's usually obvious when somebody likes you, right? If you're like most girls, you pay close attention to the signs. You notice the nuances of the way people treat you and assume they must see something positive when they react like this:

♡ Their eyes light up when they see you.

♡ They open their arms to give you a hug.

♡ They smile at you.

♡ They laugh at your jokes.

♡ They give you fist bumps and high fives.

♡ They care about your life and ask questions about what's going on.

♡ They listen intently when you speak.

♡ They say they like you.

♡ They see the best in you.

♡ They forgive your mistakes.

♡ They perk up when you're around.

♡ They love spending time with you.

It's good to notice how people treat you and to invest your time and energy in relationships that bring out your best.

But even more important than how people react to *you* is how you react to *them*.

One key truth about relationships is that people like people who like them. They're instinctively drawn to individuals who make them feel safe, protected, and accepted.

Think for a minute about how you treat others and whether your reaction invites them to draw closer or pushes them away.

♡ Are you warm and encouraging?

♡ Are you pleasant to be around?

♡ Do you wish the best for others?

♡ Do you listen more than you talk?

♡ Do you encourage people to pursue their dreams?

♡ Do you genuinely like people despite their shortcomings and flaws?

It's easy to like people when you develop a heart like Christ's. As you get closer to Him, you mature spiritually. You begin to see people as God sees them and treat them with greater love and respect.

This pleases God tremendously. It also deepens your faith. It inspires you to treat people well not to gain popularity or earn special favors, but because it feels good. That internal comfort and peace is all the reward you need.

Living Out Your Faith

We covered a lot of ground in this book, and a wide variety of topics. My greatest hope is that it has increased your confidence in both God and yourself. I pray you feel more empowered to live out your faith and to trust God's timeless truths in these key areas:

- ♡ Identity
- ♡ Confidence
- ♡ Kindness
- ♡ Character
- ♡ Commitment
- ♡ Connection
- ♡ Wisdom
- ♡ Humility
- ♡ Courage
- ♡ Direction

Even on your worst day, God loves you. Nothing you do can change His love or make you lose His approval.

And if you could see the way He looks at you, with adoring

eyes and the proud smile of a beaming Father, you'd never doubt your self-worth again. Instead, you'd joyfully run into His arms and savor the security of His love.

God has equipped you to handle the fickle nature of public opinion and to stay strong in who you are as His precious child.

And here's something for you to think about: rather than waiting for people to like you, why not like them first? Why not create that community you wish to belong to and actively engage with others by opening your heart and waiting with great expectation for God to show up?

This, my friend, is how you are designed to live: in unity with God and in community with His people. God made you for this moment in time, and as you trust Him to meet your heart's desires, you can gain the confidence to love others bravely and the freedom to accept yourself completely because your worth—and your hope—are both found in Him.

♥

Even on your worst day, God loves you.
Nothing you do can change His love
or make you lose His approval.

Notes

1. Frank Bruni, "Today's Exhausted Superkids," *The New York Times*, July 29, 2015, accessed April 24, 2016, from http://www.nytimes.com/2015/07/29/opinion/frank-bruni-todays-exhausted-superkids.html.

2. Elizabeth Bernstein, "Why Mothers and Teenage Daughters Fight," *The Wall Street Journal*, June 30, 2015, pages D1-D2, also available online at http://www.wsj.com/articles/why-mothers-and-teenage-daughters-fight-1435596179.

3. Ben Brumfield, "Selfie Named Word of the Year for 2013," *CNN Living*, November 20, 2013, accessed April 27, 2014, from http://www.cnn.com/2013/11/19/living/selfie-word-of-the-year/.

4. "Being with Someone When They Die," *Dying Matters*, accessed February 15, 2016, from http://www.dyingmatters.org/page/being-someone-when-they-die.

5. Dr. Marcellino D'Ambrosio, "Our Heart Is Restless—St. Augustine," *The Crossroads Initiative*, accessed December 28, 2015, from https://www.crossroadsinitiative.com/library_article/621/Our_Heart_Is_Restless_St_Augustine.html.

6. This definition comes from www.dictionary.com, accessed December 28, 2015, from http://dictionary.reference.com/browse/humility?s=t.

7. This quotation was posted on Facebook on August 1, 2015, on the page of Christine Caine, Public Figure, and accessed December 28, 2015, from https://www.facebook.com/theChristineCaine/photos/pb.143678730088.-2207520000.1451349038./10155975670945089/?type=3&theater.

8. This quotation was posted on Twitter on June 7, 2015, on the

account of @bobgoff, and accessed December 28, 2015, from
https://twitter.com/bobgoff/status/607548778812284928, June 7,
2015.

9. Matthew Kelley, *Rediscover Jesus* (Cincinnati, OH: Beacon
Publishing, 2015), 153.

Acknowledgments

This book exists because of the people who supported my first book.

So I'd like to start by thanking the girls who read *10 Ultimate Truths Girls Should Know*, as well as the women who gave the book to them and led small group studies in their community.

Because of you, I received an opportunity to build on that initial message. I was able to write about issues that strongly impact a girl's confidence and self-concept, such as identity, friendship, social media, and one's relationship with God. Whenever I found myself stuck in writing *Liked*, I pictured my young readers and thought about how intelligent this next generation is and how capable you girls are in taking a message and letting it shape your life. You're truly an inspiration to me.

I also want to thank the readers of my blog and newspaper column, as well as members of my Facebook and Instagram communities. Your encouragement, wisdom, and support are always perfectly timed. I'm grateful for you and this journey we're taking together.

To my agent, Andrew Wolgemuth, who wears many hats as my adviser, counselor, mediator, advocate, first reader, and legal interpreter. Andrew, you're a class act, and your ability to be professional and proactive with grace and humility is second to none. Thank you for supporting me and handling the business end with wisdom and attention to detail. I'm honored to know you and be part of your team.

Acknowledgments

To my brother, Jack Kubiszyn, who is never too busy to help his little sister. Thank you for always looking out for me and offering counsel when legal questions arise. You're the best brother, and I'm thankful for all that you and Margaret do for our family. I love you.

To my editor at Thomas Nelson, Dawn Hollomon, who made this book a collaboration from day one. Dawn, what makes you a terrific editor goes beyond talent and skills; it is the joy you add to the process. Your enthusiasm, positive attitude, and openness to my ideas have always made me feel valued and heard. Thank you for your patience and support. It's been a real pleasure to work with you.

To the incredible team at Thomas Nelson that has passionately supported *Liked*, brainstormed ideas, generated excitement, and launched it into the world: Laura Minchew, MacKenzie Howard, AnnJanette Toth, Kristen Baird, Hannah Cannon, and Katherine Dunahoo. I'm honored to be one of your authors and thankful for the friendships I've built in our common mission of empowering girls through faith. Thank you for the opportunities you provide to me and for allowing me to share in print the messages God puts on my heart.

To Mary Doyle, Sophie Hudson, and Cathy Taloe, three wonderful women who helped with manuscript questions, and to my first readers, the prayer warriors and wise souls who sharpened the manuscript: Kimberly Powell, Rachel Fry, Catherine Montgomery, Krissie Allen, Katie Houser, Mary Alice Fann, and Amy Smith. I also want to thank my writer friends, specifically Rachel Stafford, Jeannie Cunnion, Annie Pajic, Allison Hendrix, Sissy Goff, Melanie Shankle, Wynter Pitts, Renee Robinson, Courtney DeFeo, and Melanie Dale for your support, advice, and encouragement.

To Mary Frances Robertson, who helps with everything from

my children to book marketing, and always with an eager smile. You're a gift to our family and a light in our lives, and I'm so proud of who you are and who you are becoming. Thank you for being a role model and big sister to my girls. We love you, sweet girl.

To Father Bob Sullivan of St. Francis Xavier Catholic Church, who teaches me about Christ through both wisdom and example. Thank you for leading our faith community with a love that reflects God's love. Thank you, too, for your quiet acts of service behind the scenes. Your kind heart, generous spirit, and commitment to the truth make you a blessing to me and many others.

To my sisters and sisters-in-law: Krissie Allen, Dana Wolter, Mary Kathryn Gerkin, Margaret Kubiszyn, Elene Giattina, and Renee McMinn. What a blessing that I have *six outstanding women* to call family and shape the hearts of my children. Each one of you is amazing—smart, talented, loyal, and kind—and I'm thankful for your presence in my life and my family's life. You ladies are the best, and I love you.

To my mother-in-law, Becky Kampakis, and in loving memory of my father-in-law, Bubba Kampakis. Becky, it's been a difficult year with the loss of our beloved Papou. I'm so proud of you and the way you pour love into others even as you wrestle with grief. Your arms and your heart stay wide open, and what a gift it is that my family and I get to experience your warmth and devotion each day. I love you, YiaYia.

To my parents, Lucy and Jack Kubiszyn, my first and biggest fans, the ones who believe in me with unshakable faith. Thank you for affirming my worth, teaching me to be brave, and loving me through life's ups and downs. Mom, it's because of you that I became a writer, and Dad, it's because of you that I fell in love with God. I suppose that means this book is a culmination of the seeds you planted in me, seeds that I now pass on to my daughters. Thank you for loving me and my family so well. I love you both.

Acknowledgments

To my daughters, Ella, Sophie, Marie Claire, and Camille, who deepen my faith by enriching my life. You girls flood my heart with joy and gratitude. I thank God for choosing me to be your mom.

Ella, you are fourteen and growing fast. You're patient and wise, yet also animated and full of energy (especially when Shawn Mendes comes on the radio!). You're feeling the pressures of a competitive world yet navigating it beautifully as you seek to find a healthy balance between challenging yourself and leaving time for what matters most: faith, family, and friends. You are smart, grounded, and kindhearted. The character you've developed—along with your many talents—will take you far in life, so stay close to God and let Him guide your choices. Remember, His plan for you is perfect.

Sophie, you are eleven and as strong, brave, and smart as ever. Once you set your mind on something, you're unstoppable. Your passion for people, extroverted personality, and loyalty to your friends have helped you build great relationships, yet your best relationship is the quiet one you have with God, which runs deeply in your heart. Keep your faith strong, keep your eyes fixed on Jesus, and trust God's mighty plans for you. Know, too, that you inspire me to be strong and brave and to love others as fiercely as you do.

Marie Claire, you are ten and radiant with joy. Your kindness, compassion, and tender heart make you a dear friend to many. You love people for who they are, and you offer them a safe place to be themselves. On top of this, you're hard-working, motivated, and smart. I can't wait to see what God has in store for you, and I love seeing Him work through you already in your gentle spirit, contagious laughter, and profound insights. You are a blessing, my angel. Keep your heart open to God, and let His light continue to shine through you.

Acknowledgments

Camille, you are six and smart as a whip. You draw our family closer through our shared love for you. While it's hard to watch my baby grow up, it's also fun because you are rocking it! You love elementary school and are thrilled to be with your sisters. You're growing by leaps and bounds, and you've hit your stride in expanding your mind, your heart, and your friendships. Let God continue to do this great work He's started in you. Always keep your energy, sense of humor, and love for life—and trust God to use these beautiful gifts to impact those around you.

And to my husband Harry, my best friend and soul mate, who teaches me more about the love of Christ than anyone else on earth. By loving and accepting the real me, you give me the courage to be real with others. I pray that our daughters and the girls in their generation will find someone who makes them feel as cherished, secure, and protected as you make me feel. Thank you for your commitment to me and to our family. I love you and this life we've created together.

And to Christ the Savior, my ultimate Joy. All good things come from You, and all peace is possible through You. Thank You for bringing light, hope, and salvation to a broken and imperfect world. Thank You for Your grace and mercy. To God be the honor and glory.

About the Author

Kari Kubiszyn Kampakis is a blogger, author, speaker, and newspaper columnist from Birmingham, Alabama. Her first book, *10 Ultimate Truths Girls Should Know*, has been used widely across the country by teen youth groups and small groups to empower girls through faith.

Kari's work has been featured on *The Huffington Post*, *TODAY Parents*, and other national outlets. She and her husband, Harry, have four daughters and a dog named Lola. Learn more by visiting www.karikampakis.com or finding Kari on Facebook, Instagram, Pinterest, and Twitter.

Also from Kari Kampakis

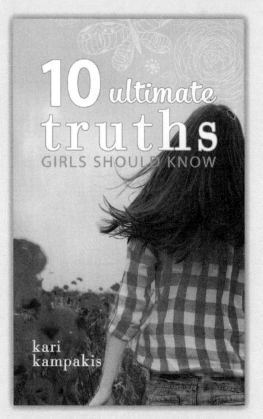

$\mathcal{W}$ith practical advice, loving support, and insightful discussion questions, *10 Ultimate Truths Girls Should Know* will help you become the young woman God created you to be. These 10 truths include:

- People peak at different times in life. Trust God's plan for you.
- Get comfortable with being uncomfortable. Otherwise you'll never stick to your guns.
- Today's choices set the stage for your reputation.
- You were born to fly.

Available wherever books are sold.